WHAT YOU DON'T KNOW CAN BE FATAL

REVELATIONS THAT CHANGED MY LIFE

PASTOR AL GEE

Copyright © 2015 by Al Gee

All rights reserved. This book is protected by the copyright laws of the United States of America. This book may not be copied or reprinted for commercial gain or profit. The use of short quotations or occasional page copying for personal or group study is permitted and encouraged. Permission will be granted upon request.

Printed in the United States of America

CONTENTS

Foreword by Pastor Andy Thompson	5
Introduction	7
Section One: Taking My City For God	**9**
Chapter 1: May I Introduce You To…GOD?	13
Chapter 2: What You Don't Know Can Be Fatal	19
Chapter 3: Believing Is Seeing	23
Chapter 4: B.Y.O.F (Build Your Own Faith)	27
Section Two: My Journey	**33**
Chapter 5: Wake Up! Sin Is Not Your Problem	35
Chapter 6: Trials Don't Come To Make You Strong	41
Chapter 7: Treat Sickness Like You Treat Sin	45
Section Three: Entering My Dark Place	**49**
Chapter 8: The Fault Of Finding Fault	53
Chapter 9: Strife: Satan's Perfect Spoiler	55
Chapter 10: Procrastination: The Silent Destroyer	59
Chapter 11: Neglect: The Thief Of Future Blessings	63
Chapter 12: Be Bitter Or Get Better	65
Section Four: My Consolation	**69**
Chapter 13: How Can I Hear The Voice Of God	71
Chapter 14: Hearing Is Not Enough	77
Chapter 15: Wavering Disqualifies Your Prayer	81
Chapter 16: Why Are You Asking For What's Already Yours	83
Chapter 17: Before	87

Chapter 18: You Are What You Eat ... 91
Chapter 19: Change Your Words, Change Your World ... 95

Section Five: Secret Seduction, Public Pain ... 97
Chapter 20: God Ain't Doing Nothing More About The Devil ... 101
Chapter 21: Blessings Don't Fall Like Cherries ... 105
Chapter 22: The Sucker Punch ... 111
Chapter 23: God Isn't Obligated To Bless You Where He Didn't Send You ... 115
Chapter 24: Be Prepared For The Counter Attack ... 117

Section Six: When My Faith Held ... 121
Chapter 25: Why Aren't You Receiving? ... 123
Chapter 26: Beware Of The Faith Look Alike ... 127
Chapter 27: Fear Contaminates Faith ... 129
Chapter 28: The Master Key: Controlling Your Thoughts ... 133
Chapter 29: Permission Granted ... 137

Section Seven: I'm Giving You Back 20 Years ... 143
Chapter 30: Forgiveness Ensures The Flow Of Power ... 145
Chapter 31: The Power Of "Now" ... 147
Chapter 32: Receive Now ... 151

Section Endnotes ... 153

FOREWORD

The Prophet Hosea spoke a word that still reverberates through the Body of Christ; a concept that I am not sure we have truly grasped; but one, nevertheless, that still affects and infects many believers. He said quite simply: "My people are destroyed for a lack of knowledge."

That phrase says volumes and would take hours to analyze. One of the greatest lessons I have learned in leading and pastoring—now for 25 years—is this: People do what they are TAUGHT to do. Every one of us is a sum total of words that have been spoken over us, about us, and into us. To change your life, your actions, your perspective; you have to first change the words that surround you.

With those thoughts in mind, allow me to recommend Pastor Al Gee as an excellent teacher who will reconfigure some of the misperceptions, reeducate your mis-education, and will put you on a path to life.

There is nothing like a teacher who will not only give instruction, but will also share from their own experience; who will become transparent, and help you see something from their own victories and defeats. To be taught by someone that not only practices what he preaches, but also preaches what he practices: that is truly a unique opportunity. Grasp that opportunity right now. Get into this book, because the right words can change your life. Fight the good fight of Faith—fight to take hold of the eternal life to which you were called. Seek first the knowledge of the Kingdom, and EVERYTHING will be added unto you!

Pastor Andy Thompson,
Senior Pastor
World Overcomers Christian Church
Durham, NC

INTRODUCTION

I understand that en route to the invention of the light bulb, Thomas Edison had hundreds of failures. Instead of giving up, he viewed each failure as one more hindrance out of the way, on his road to his success. From each one, Edison learned a lesson and used it as a stepping-stone to his goal. My life with God has been similar.

From the first day of my salvation, I focused on the goal of living in daily victory. The enemy had other things in mind. He set about to make sure that either through traditional, religious thinking; persistent personality flaws; or by the sheer number of my failures, he would somehow prevent me. And, because of his determination, I have encountered many crippling hindrances. Some were setbacks that could easily be corrected with a change of my behavior; others took long, hot, dry seasons to overcome. And still, others were so subtle that I wasn't even aware there was a real problem, that is, until God's promised results didn't occur. I discovered a veritable arsenal of weaponry that was created and designed to ruin my hopes and dreams. To God's glory, each one, though intended to cause irreparable harm, became a life lesson.

I would have preferred for someone to pull me aside, at the beginning of my ministry, and pour this knowledge into me. I believe that would have saved me time and hurt. But this wasn't the case. My leaders taught me all they knew. It just so happened that the entire focus of ministry was changing; even as I was learning from their old notes. As sincere as I was in my approach to ministry, I discovered that on some important concepts, I was sincerely wrong. And on others, I just didn't know enough.

Blindsided by this unflattering revelation, my pride was broken into little pieces. And what I found was merely the typical prelude to real growth. God started from that point, teaching me the things you're about to read. Some are brief explanations of misconceptions I had learned as truth; others are revelations critical to your sustained progress and growth as a believer.

THANK GOD FOR THE RAVENS!

The way God sent this information to me was quite unorthodox. Much like Elijah's provision from the ravens in 1 Kings 17:6, my provisions too arrived in unexpected ways. As I stated, I would have preferred a mentor to guide me and answer my concerns as they surfaced. Instead, through books; tapes; seminars; teachings; and new acquaintances, answers and corrections came. Kenneth Hagin, Chuck Swindoll, R.W. Schambach, Mike Murdoch, Marilyn Hickey, Joyce Meyers, Richard Briley, E.W. Kenyon, F.F. Bosworth, Watchman Nee, and dozens more: all were used by the Lord in getting the truth to me. As I think about it, what a miracle it was that each time I was in urgent need, answers in these various forms would mysteriously appear.

When I learned what I was doing wrong, the light came. I couldn't wait to share what I had learned with those experiencing similar predicaments. It is my hope that this writing will help you to be aware of the enemy's devices. These are at the very least some mistakes to not make, and some roads to not take. The dictionary's definition of a revelation is "a dramatic disclosure of something not previously known." It took years for me to learn the simple insights you're about to read. I rejoice to be able to make the road a little easier and shorter for you.

Some of these concepts, I'm sure you already know; but it will be useful to revisit them from a slightly different perspective. I have only dealt briefly with each revelation I have learned. Any serious student of the Word will dig deeper and find more information on the subjects brought out here. I don't recommend that you read this book straight through in one sitting, or that you read the chapters in any particular order. Whatever your style or method of reading, may these pages enrich your life; save you countless hours; and help you in your path to

SECTION ONE

TAKING MY CITY FOR GOD

From 1977 to 1994, I was the pastor of a small denominational, storefront church of approximately 50 members in Omaha, Nebraska. For some pastors, that's a big congregation; but starting out at age 27, I had a vision of taking the entire city for God! Being taught to fast, pray, work hard, and live holy, I committed wholeheartedly to it. My mentors admonished me that if I did that, God would do the rest. I did, but the results I desired never happened. If fasting, praying, etc. were the keys to success, the city would have been mine. But accomplishing what I desired required much more. That fact was soon painfully etched into my life.

I made sure that my members and I did monthly consecrations (fasting and praying), including all night prayers and public street meetings—complete with bullhorn and tambourines. (I never let on, but I didn't enjoy being a public spectacle.) It involved singing songs (without music) and preaching on the street. The few brave souls that typically showed up looked inadequate, but as their leader, I had to do what I believed had to be done no matter what. I would pick the worst street we could find, where there was a lot of ungodly activity going on. That was the well-earned reputation of 24th Street. And it definitely lived up to its reputation.

One day as I was preaching hell-fire and brimstone, a man got so angry that he stopped his car and got out. He looked to be about 6ft 5in, weighing about 270lbs, and had obviously been drinking. He stormed his way up to me and angrily demanded that I "shut up and stop preaching that mess." His facial expression showed that he had every intention of doing me bodily harm if I didn't comply. Of course I prayed, but I didn't know what to do next. Up to that time, I had never thought about the possibility of being assaulted for the gospel. As he came near, another man—seemingly out of nowhere—stepped between us. This was obviously someone he knew, who motioned with wielding hands for him to calm down. To my utter surprise, and relief, the irate man stopped his ranting, returned to his car and sped away. To me, that meant that God was with me.

During my time pastoring, scores of people were saved and lives were changed for the better. However, to my great disappointment, the church never grew beyond *fifty* members. Why were we not exploding with souls?

I could not explain it. I cried out to the Lord in anguish, pleading for an explanation for my dilemma. I was desperate for a breakthrough, but for some reason unbeknownst to me, God was not in a hurry to give it. He took his sweet time.

I found out years later, this was never about me growing a large church. It was about me learning some harsh realities, while unlearning some stubborn misconceptions. I would just have to dry my tears, adjust my vision, and make up my mind to humbly learn the lessons this prolonged period of disappointment was sure to teach me.

CHAPTER ONE

MAY I INTRODUCE YOU TO... GOD?

"Jesus answered, 'Have I been so long time with you, and yet hast thou not known me, Phillip? He that hath seen me hath seen the Father.'"

-John 14:9

"The thief cometh not but for to steal and to kill and to destroy; I am come that they may have life, and that they might have it more abundantly."

-John 10:10

Your concept of God affects everything. How you view him determines whether you live fully surrounded in an eternal, loving embrace; or whether you spend each day looking over your shoulder, anticipating sudden calamity. It's difficult to love God if you feel he's out to (as the old folks used to say) "catch you with your works undone." Hell would certainly be our home if he caught us with our works undone. As a result, for years we nervously watched the sky, thinking that at any moment Jesus could return and we would be caught out of his will. "You're gonna bust hell wide open" -- was the phrase the preachers used. I have always been more afraid of what God could do to me, than enamored with what he's done for me. This perspective came directly from what I was taught about God. As the descendants of slaves, we started out viewing God as our Master. Old Testament teachings reinforced the notion that he could not be approached without great fear and trembling. Thank God for the teachings of Jesus. He came teaching that we should call him our Father or "Daddy."

Knowledge about God is cumulative. As time has elapsed, we have learned more and more about him. Little by little, we get a clearer picture of a God who is love. Years ago in Washington, DC, I was teaching along the lines of the great blessings God has bestowed upon his children. A young woman asked to speak with me afterwards. She was in a quandary. The very ministry I was teaching in, taught its members that God was about to bring judgment upon the earth, and that none would escape. How could she relax and love a God who was lying in wait to bring destruction upon the world? The best I could do was to show her the scriptures that give us further revelation of God. However, from that time on, it was apparent to me that many believers needed to be formally reintroduced to …God.

BLAMING GOD

The world has always been convinced that God is behind the fury of destructive hurricanes, whose cyclonic winds storm and reduce thriving communities to heaps of scattered debris; and the frightening tsunami, which carries in its towering tidal waves, screaming women and children; and the terrifying tornadoes, striking suddenly at night with only the telltale sound of an oncoming locomotive before total calamity; and the devastating earthquakes, which in minutes leave entire regions in ruins.

Long ago, we resigned to the belief that this is somehow God's divine right: to unleash mayhem upon mankind any time he wills. He is God, and this is one reason why many fear him. But, we are often overwhelmed at the magnitude of the devastation that comes without warning. It is both violent and sensational, destroying lives and livelihoods, like a predator hungry for the taste of wreck and ruin. Death and fear are co-conspirators on these rampages, stalking and devouring their victims with wanton disregard for the precious life of even the sweetest little child. Consequently, only those "lucky" enough to not be in the wrong place at the wrong time, survive. This begs the question— "How can a loving God do such things to his children?"

CHILDHOOD BELIEFS

From childhood, we have believed that only God is powerful enough to control the unpredictable patterns of weather. As a young boy growing up in Florida, I was told to sit still when we heard the thunder because God was doing his business. I've always been taught that God is in charge of storms, and that everything, ultimately, goes according to his divine plan. But that's more than a little disturbing. That would mean that the mother whose children were swept from her arms by surging floodwaters; and the father who lost his wife and children when the mudslide covered his village; and the child whose parents succumbed to the cholera that followed in the wake of earthquake's carnage; were all affected by the actions of a God who controlled and regulated everything. But there is a better explanation. Jesus implied in the scripture above—"if you really want to see how God acts: look at me. I don't steal, kill or destroy. Just the opposite… I came to give you life to the fullest."

LIMITED KNOWLEDGE OF SATAN

Job, who seemed to have little or no knowledge of the devil, said: "the Lord gives and the Lord takes away, blessed be the name of the Lord." Many of us have thought that way about God. Our traditional interpretation of Job's plight was that it was one of an unwitting victim. In light of his circumstances, we mistakenly infer that our status here on earth is nothing more than that of pawns, in the great chess game between God and Satan. As such, at any time, we may be used in a contest, which may wreak havoc in our lives because we are clueless to what is going on.

Worse still, is the troubling thought that we really have no say in the matter. If God is in the mood for a wager with Satan, like it or not, mankind will be forced to participate in the game. But even the most ardent proponent of this line of thinking must have observed two completely different lifestyles of Job. The difference is obvious between the blessed lifestyle Job had with God, and the cursed one he had when Satan was allowed to come near and touch his life. With God, the blessings; prosperity; and favor abounded; with Satan, death; sickness; and loss prevailed. In Satan, is death and sickness. It is his calling card, his MO or modus operandi.

GOD GETS THE BLAME

Job blamed God for whatever happened in his life, whether good or bad. There is very little mention of Satan in the whole of the Old Testament.

Besides the coup he successfully executed against Adam and Eve in the Garden, he gets very little mention, which is probably what he preferred. For centuries, he has remained hidden, able to do his devilish work, while God has gotten the blame. He could do his most effective work: killing, stealing, and destroying; and the people would attribute all of it to God. Jesus came to clear up this centuries old misconception, and to introduce the entire world to the real God. Jesus makes a distinct separation to clear up the ancient way of viewing God as a stern, self-absorbed, unyielding, unforgiving tyrant, by saying: "the thief comes to steal, kill and destroy but I've come to give you life to the fullest." He said: "When you see me you're seeing your Father." He's behind the scene doing the works that we see Jesus perform.

THE HEART OF THE MATTER

There is one miracle achieved by Jesus that places into perspective the world of difference between God and the enemy: It's the one when Jesus rebuked the wind and calmed the sea.[1] Jesus was on his way to the region of the Gadarenes. We find out later that he is on his way to rid the region of a monster of a man who is possessed with demons. He boards a ship and goes to sleep. Suddenly, a furious storm arises and waves begin to fill the ship with water. His disciples, some of whom are experienced seaworthy fishermen, panic at the severity of this storm. It must have been ferocious, something completely out of the ordinary. Fearing for their very lives, they desperately wake Jesus to help them. Jesus then does something that totally shocks their collective mindsets: he actually rebukes the wind and calms the sea! No man had ever done such a mighty act! Since this is Jesus, every experienced reader of the Bible feels that he's just doing what he has the power to do. It's no stretch for us to see him do such things. Those of us who have read the Bible, know that he also raised the dead and came back from the dead, and are not surprised. However, there is a surprise in this act.

If we say that God is in control, and that God is the one who controls storms and all spectacular weather events, we just witnessed Jesus rebuking something that God sent. If Jesus rebuked what God sent, the kingdom is divided, and as Jesus said: "it cannot stand." No, quite the contrary, Jesus was not rebuking something God sent. He was rebuking something sent by Satan to hinder and stop their progress. In this one act, he exposes who is actually working behind the scenes.

Satan was behind this storm. Jesus was coming to deliver and convert their demonic champion—the monster of the Gadarenes: the demon possessed man who had been the object of fear and fright throughout the region. This was a preemptive move against Jesus but it fell short. Also demonstrated was the authority believers have in the earth.

THE TRUTH OF THE MATTER ON STORMS

The truth of the matter is that in the beginning God gave man dominion over the earth. Adam lost it to Satan and fell from his original state. Since the fall, Satan became the god of this world (II Cor. 4:4). He was successful in the coup that deposed Adam from his God-given authority over the earth. Satan has now taken the reigns and uses what was meant to bless mankind, for his own destructive purposes.

That's why the earth and the entire physical universe, since that time, have been under a curse. This curse expanded to the very throne room where prayers are answered. For when Daniel prayed, the angel reported that his prayer was heard in heaven, but was hindered by Satan.[2] **THEREFORE, THE LAWS THAT LARGELY GOVERN THE EARTH TODAY CAME ABOUT AS A RESULT OF THE CURSE, AND FROM THE FALL OF MAN.** As a result, the storms; floods; and tornadoes that tear up the landscape, and the droughts that dry up the vegetation, causing famine, did not come from God, but from the Fall. So the destructive events that we ascribe to God are not his doing. They are known in the business world as acts of God, but they are not from God. Satan is their author: stealing, killing and destroying are his calling card. We must get this fact into our thinking. If we want to get a look at God's ways and personality, look at Jesus. The miracles he performed, and the words he said, all came from the Father God. Jesus didn't make people sick—he healed the sick. He wasn't ruthless and cruel in his dealings toward man—but loving and forgiving. He was the one who told us to call upon God our *Father*, when we pray. Jesus lived and ultimately died to demonstrate the difference between God and Satan.

Let us therefore make the same distinction the Bible makes: God is not making people sick, or destroying property; nor does he live in or send terrifying storms. God so *loved* the world that he gave his only begotten son…When Satan is finally removed from human interaction, the Bible describes that there will be no more crying, no more dying, and no more pain. When he is removed, all the miseries of mankind will forever cease. This makes it obvious that Satan is the author of sickness, destruction and death. Thank God we have power over all the work of the enemy! Let's do the works of Jesus, and go about to destroy the destructive works of the enemy.

CHAPTER TWO

WHAT YOU DON'T KNOW CAN BE FATAL

"My people are destroyed for the lack of knowledge."
-Hosea 4:6

Lack of knowledge is fatal to the child of God. God himself knows that the destruction of his people can be traced directly to this deficiency. Lack of knowledge makes victims of those who were designed by God to be victors in every area of life.

Many years ago, as a young man, I heard in a Sunday message, a story that so moved me that it is yet imprinted in my memory. It was a story of a woman and her small child, who on a cold wintry day boarded a train, destined to meet family and friends. While onboard, she inquired about her destination, and was given incorrect information, from a well-meaning individual, about the correct stop. Immediately upon hearing what she thought was her destination being called, she gathered her child and her belongings. She then made a hasty path to the platform between the cars, and with some effort, managed to carefully navigate the steep stairs to the pavement below. Only after the train pulled off did she realize her mistake. She had gotten off in the wrong town. Her destination was miles up the track. Worse still, was the fact that there was no one at the station, and no one in sight. Tragically, the cruel price to be exacted for her innocent mistake would shock and horrify townsfolk throughout the region for years to come. She was found at the station, but much too late, huddled together with her child, frozen to death. She and her precious child were the victims of wrong information. The sermon that followed was appropriately titled, "Victims of the Wrong Information." All of the good intentions in the world cannot make up for the tragedies that befall believers every day, due to their lack of knowledge. God said that his people are "destroyed" because of it.

It is so frustrating, looking for God to do something that just doesn't come to pass, especially when we earnestly believe that his own words obligate him to perform it. For years, as a pastor, I expected God to do certain things, simply because he was God and I was his servant. I didn't understand why sickness persisted, as well as lack of finances. It was my belief that because I lived a separated life, the rest was to fall in place as fringe benefits. I fasted for days, and prayed for hours at a time. In the Pentecostal church I attended, we rejoiced, shouted, and danced before the Lord. But none of these actions yielded anything more than temporary relief. The most we experienced was short-lived miracles and "faith accidents," which were results that occurred without us understanding why they had occurred; and, without us knowing how to repeat them. It was then that I learned that some things cannot come as a result of a church worship service, or as a result of simply the laying on of hands: they only come through the studying of, and feeding on, the Word of God.

GOD DOES EVERYTHING BY HIS WORD

Anyone desiring to know God, and wanting to walk with him, must take time to study his Word. Why? Because God does everything by his Word. The scriptures declare that he sent his Word and healed them.[3] His Word is the essence of who he is. In the beginning was the Word, and the Word was with God, and the Word was God. Nothing was created without it.[4] It's our understanding that the universe was framed by his Word.[5]

God is a God of principles and laws. These principles are so real and powerful that great care must be taken in using them. **THE SAME PRINCIPLE THAT BRINGS THE DIVINE POWER OF GOD, WILL IN TURN KEEP YOU OUT OF THE RESULTS IF NOT FOLLOWED PROPERLY.** Anyone desiring to walk with God and wanting to enjoy his benefits, must be a student of his Word. Discover the power of his Word and you will discover the creative force that formed the universe, and continues its expansion up to this day.

SLAVES AND STRANGERS

The Bible states that although we may have the legal right to the whole fortune of being an heir of the King of Glory, if we are children (immature in knowledge and wisdom), we are no different than slaves.[6] What a statement! It also describes the quality of life of many believers today living in cruel bondage like slaves. Any believer not knowing the Word of God, suffers the same fate. Not that God is punishing him or her, but that lack of knowledge of the Word severely robs their quality of life.

Paul, in Ephesians 2:12, describes our plight when we didn't know Christ, and were as "aliens from the commonwealth of Israel, and strangers from the covenants of promise." Sadly, this is also a description of the believer who is unaware of their covenant with God. He is a "stranger" and an "alien," or foreigner, to the things of God that are designed for blessing his life. In that same verse, that person is described as being "without hope".

WORDS ARE REAL THINGS TO GOD

In order to know the power of the Word, we must understand the way God operates. As a creator, he used his words to cause things to come to pass. It appears that God considers his word an actual living thing. He said in Isaiah 55:11 that his word would not return to him void, but rather accomplish that which he pleases. On the other hand, man, who fell from his privileged position long ago, lost this high regard for words. A word spoken by God is the actual thing to God. When God gives his word, that's the launching of the thing you need. Satan cannot reverse the word once it has gone out of the mouth of God. Therefore, God uses that pattern over and over again.

Natural, physical ways of creating things are subject to interference by the enemy, who is the god of this world system.[7] The natural process is subject to weather conditions, circumstances, and outward forces. The Word of God is not subject to the physical realm. It is a

He spoke to the wind.[8] He spoke and said "Let there be light." In order that Jesus could be born of a virgin, the angel spoke words to Mary. We use words for many things, but we lost their original meaning and power.

HIS WAYS

"My thoughts are not your thoughts, neither are your ways my ways…"
-Isaiah 55:8

"They do always err in their heart; and they have not known my ways."
-Hebrews 3:10

For the most part, we don't consider something as real unless we can observe it physically. There are many things which we cannot see, but still use every day—e.g. the air we breathe. Much too often, we are expecting God to deliver a physical thing, when he is perfectly satisfied with giving us a word. Doesn't he know we need the physical thing? Why does he frustrate us with a word when we need a thing? Once again, as a thoughtful Father, he is taking us back to the way all physical things are made. Each manifestation starts with a word. Our heavenly Father is re-teaching his children the kingdom principles—the principles that accompany our authority. It's great to have a meal that someone else prepared; it's better to know how to prepare the meal yourself, so that you can continue the process at will. Remember the old wise saying, "If you give a man a fish you feed him for a day. If you teach him how to fish, he can feed himself for a lifetime."? Whatever the amount of time and effort needed to initiate and complete the process, by which things are created, it's time and energy well spent.

Cut man off from the Word of God, and you will have essentially neutralized him, and restricted him to the realm of feeling and natural intellect. In doing so, God is also prevented from blessing man the way he intended. "Man shall not live by bread alone but by every word that proceedeth out from the mouth of God…"[9] Lack of knowledge, or ignorance of the Word, strikes a lethal blow to a prosperous relationship with our Father.

CHAPTER THREE

BELIEVING IS SEEING

"Seeing is believing," people say, not realizing that such a harmless statement is full of doubt, and misses the things of God by miles. The truth is just the opposite: believing is seeing. Here is a classic case of believing by the senses, in the words of Thomas the disciple:

In John 20:25, Thomas said:

"Except I shall see in his hands the print of the nails, and put my finger into the print of the nails, and thrust my hand into his side, I will not believe."

Maybe after the horrific events of the crucifixion of Jesus, Thomas was taking no chances in authenticating the real Jesus. Unwisely, he reverted to his pre-Jesus mentality, departing from the many faith lessons he had learned from the master. Losing precious faith ground, he reverted to preferring physical evidence. Having been up close with Jesus for three years, he learned that nothing of significance originates in the natural physical world—everything is orchestrated by the Spirit. But, in fairness to Thomas, if we had all experienced the ordeal he had just endured, we might have responded in the same manner. He had just witnessed his Lord and Savior being arrested; wounded; bruised; and beaten by Roman soldiers, then dragged through a jeering crowd, carrying his wooden death bed—a cross—and finally, cruelly fastened to that cross, with metal spikes driven through his hands and feet. Who among us would not have been totally shaken by such a spectacle? That does not negate the fact that faith, real faith, is not of the physical senses. In verse 29, Jesus said to him:

> "Thomas because thou hast seen me, thou hast believed: blessed are they that have not seen, and yet have believed."

BELIEVING FROM THE SENSES

I dare say that anyone who believes from the five senses—totally relying on only what they can physically taste, smell, hear, see, or touch—is in for lots of frustration. The journey from following the senses to believing the word of God, and living by faith, must be made. We have been trained over the years, to use our five senses skillfully to detect just about everything. But when it comes to God, and the things of God, this way does not work. Our origin is spiritual. We are made in the likeness and image of God, who is a spirit.[10] Our father God has given his spirit and his Word to teach us his ways—the ways of the spirit. We must cooperate and learn. This is not accomplished without some difficulty, because we have spent years learning the ways of fallen man, who was cut off from his spiritual heritage. But since Jesus came, "old things are passed away and all things are become new."[11] He cannot allow us to continue to stumble through life limited by the experiences of the natural physical senses. The physical body cannot contact or communicate with God. It was never designed that way. It is designed to be our earthly house only.[12]

No matter how unfamiliar we are with this, we must move beyond the limitations of the natural. Jesus said that if we have faith as a grain of mustard seed, we can speak to the mountains and they will obey and nothing will be impossible to us.[13] We must get familiar with receiving without seeing; that's the more perfect way of the spirit. Jesus said in Mark 11:24, "...when you pray, believe you receive and you shall have." This is quite different from what we're used to, but in order to live like Jesus, we must have a good grasp of it.

"FOR WE WALK BY FAITH AND NOT BY SIGHT"[14]

Living by our physical senses is very limiting to us as believers. God is so far above the limitations of the physical world that it takes faith to please him.[15] Our bodies are constantly sending signals to our brains about everything they are experiencing. They were not designed to rule us, but to obey us. The Word of God is to be the determining factor in every situation for the believer. When we experience symptoms of sickness, we must believe the report of Isaiah 53:4 which states that "he bore our sicknesses and carried our infirmities." If *he* bore them and carried them, *we* don't have to. We must take the Word of God like medicine, every few hours, in order to experience healing. His words are life and health (medicine) to every part of our bodies.[16]

Abraham believed God and considered not his own body, but was strong in faith giving glory to God.[17] Because of that, he was the type of individual who God could use mightily: someone who believed God in the way God desired to be trusted—believing beyond the senses. He believed God when everything in his physical body was contrary to what he believed. As a result, he received what was promised and much more. God promised him that his offspring would be as numerous as the grains of sand on the seashore. To this very day, all who believe beyond the physical senses are called the children of Abraham.[18]

FLEECES ARE UNRELIABLE

In our day, putting out a fleece (a wooly sheep coat) is a sure way to "get fleeced." In the Book of Judges, Chapter 6, Gideon created a precedent when he decided to let God prove that he (Gideon) had been chosen—despite being a lowly farmer's son—to deliver Israel from its enemies.[19] God miraculously made Gideon's fleece wet and the ground dry, and according to Gideon's request the next day, he caused the ground to be wet and the fleece dry. This was the proof Gideon needed that God was indeed sending him forth. He ultimately defeated an army too numerous to count with only 300 men.

Christians, encouraged by Gideon's success, have since made attempts at obtaining the same proofs, by putting out some sort of "fleece" before God. For example, one might say, "Lord, if it's your will that I marry Mr. X, please send a flock of birds into my backyard this morning." If the flock flew into their backyard that morning, they married Mr. X.

Expecting God to respond this way is asking for disaster. For the New Testament believers—that's us—God has a better way. He is presently leading by the Spirit. To try to get him to return to this Old Testament pattern of performing something detectable to the senses, is to regress. God is going to lead by his spirit. Answers and leading will come from the spirit of God into Man's spirit. Proverbs 20:27 says that "the spirit of man is the candle of the Lord." Physical manifestations will come as a result.

Pressing God for a manifestation in the physical, to prove anything, can become a setback to your faith. It can move you backward from seeing what you believe, to believing only what you see. It can set you back for years in the development of stronger faith. God is teaching you to believe even though you do not see. This strengthens our ability to live beyond the seen realm, taking us into the realm of faith. There the enemy is totally defeated. Trying to get God to perform something in the physical realm so you can believe, is a costly mistake. How many people have lost the victory because the pain of an illness didn't immediately subside? Their victory was lost when they said, in accordance with what they sensed physically, "I didn't get my healing."

Even some preachers, known for exceptional faith, have wept bitterly after conducting healing meetings for "those who didn't receive anything," despite Matthew 7:8 clearly stating that "everyone who asks receives." Sadly, God was counting on them to maintain their faith in the unseen, over a period of time, in order to release healing for the ones who were too weak in faith to believe they had received.

In this world of fallen man, we continue to put the cart before the horse. Charles Capps, a prominent faith teacher, said: "We keep saying what we have (in the physical realm) instead of having what we say."

As the rain and snow come down from heaven, and waters the earth causing it to bring forth and bud, so does the Word of God water the natural realm.[20] God's Word will change the natural realm, but faith doesn't wait until the change is detected by the senses to believe it is so. Faith lays claim at the time the promise is heard and grasped.

CHAPTER FOUR

B.Y.O.F (BUILD YOUR OWN FAITH)

It is better for you to fall on your face continually using your faith, than to proceed up the road of your life accomplishing significant achievements without it. Because inevitably there will come a day when you will face a challenge that cannot be won without faith. But if you keep using your faith, one day the enemy will challenge you, and you will rise to the occasion and knock him totally out of contention.[21]

It's a mistake to believe that you can ride other people's faith for too long. God expects each individual to take time to develop his or her own faith. We are all at some point required to display the ability to believe, in the midst of contradictory circumstances, and to prove that we actually own that which we cannot see. God gives all of us ample time to do just that. He often waits for years—a considerable length of time to build up our faith stamina. When we neglect to do so, the consequences can be more than disturbing; blessings can be forfeited, lives can be lost, and desperately needed results can go missing.

GODLY PARENTS

Because their parents are in the ministry, and moved in the power of God, the children of some ministers believe that mom and dad will always be able to pray them out of any trouble, and get them healed. Kenneth Hagin shared how although he had always prayed and experienced the healing of his children, a time came when his prayers didn't work. His son had an affliction, and as usual, Kenneth prayed against it, expecting his son to be fully healed as all the other times before. But it didn't happen; the affliction remained. After inquiring of God as to why, the Lord explained that when his son was younger he was allowed to carry him, but his son was now at the age when he was required to have his own faith; Kenneth would no longer be allowed to carry him. God graciously allows both biological and spiritual parents to carry the newborns for a while—interceding for them, praying for them, and watching for their souls. But there comes a time when these parents have to let go, and let their children grow up. Spiritual maturity should be the goal of all believers. We are to grow up in him and mature. One critical aspect of that growth is building faith to the point of being effective and getting results.

ANOINTED MINISTERS

Church members, who in the past were healed miraculously by the prayer of an anointed man or woman of God, when facing another illness will return to that powerful minister expecting the same results. They erroneously conclude, when that same outcome doesn't occur, that the minister has lost his/her anointing. They recount the past, reminiscing the miracles of old times when "the power of God fell mightily." Sadly, they have miss the opportunity to learn the Word and build-up their own faith. God is so merciful; he gives plenty of time—in some cases years and decades—for people to learn and to build-up their faith. When they don't, they easily succumb to the attack of the enemy, who is more than willing to drive them to an early end, causing them to depart this life much earlier than they should have, without ever having experienced God's best here in the earth.

POWERFUL MEETINGS

There have been meetings where the worship service was so high, and the presence of God so strong, that miracles began to happen, including healings and powerful demonstrations of the spirit. This is a corporate anointing generated by the faith of all those in attendance. So strong and powerful is that atmosphere that God is free to bless in unusual ways; and he takes advantage of the opportunity to bless his people. But the church gets a bad mark when people who have received miraculous demonstrations, leave the meeting and gradually lose what they so powerfully received. The doubters pounce on this weakness, and declare "It's all a hoax!" when miracles are short lived. The truth of the matter is that even though miracles occur in special worship services, each individual is expected—once on their own—to build his own foundation of faith on the Word of God. What we receive in the congregation, among lots of believers, certainly will not last when you're on your own without faith. However, loss can be a thing of the past if we learn to believe God for ourselves. No one can please God without faith, and he that wavers when praying cannot receive anything from the Lord.

THE GIFTED AND ANOINTED ARE NOT EXEMPT

Anointed preachers and evangelists are used in powerful ways to heal and bless God's people. However, they should know that being gifted and anointed does not replace, or negate, the requirement to build their faith. Too many have relied on their anointing to carry them through storms of problems and sicknesses. It's a rude awakening to find that gifting and anointing are no substitute for honing faith skills, even for ministers and spiritual leaders. To please God, we must believe when we can't see; trust him when all physical evidence is contrary to what we are praying for. We must believe God and know that sickness cannot stay, though it may come our way. Each of us, after some time, is required to be able to use the "substance of things hoped for and the evidence of things not seen" to get what we need in this life. It is sad to see people, known for great healing revivals, die of horrible infirmities. Regrettably, some did not take time to build their faith to the level needed when the attacks came close to home, on their very own bodies.

OLDER BELIEVERS

It's also equally sad when people who have lived for the Lord all their lives are confronted late in life with storms, from which they seemingly never recover. Why? Some mistakenly believed that church membership and attendance would somehow be enough to carry them through any trial. They were doing the work of the church, but never took the time to build faith for what was to come. Their lives are filled with gospel music, and religious clichés like "God is able," "the Lord knows all things," and "God is in control," when all these were merely facades to cover up the fact that their faith remained "little faith."

By no means am I diminishing the great accomplishments of those who have carried the banner in the heat of the day and persevered. Nor can I criticize their great commitment. I long to see older believers leave this life in glory and not fear; in blessing and strength, instead of weakness and lack. Let's all fight this good fight of faith and die believing God, but not in fear—cowering in the presence of an enemy who has taken advantage of our lack of faith.

Faith has been described as a muscle that needs nourishment and exercise. It is fed by hearing the Word of God, and exercised by speaking words and acting on the Word. When the threat of a terminal illness attacks, that's not the best time to begin to strengthen faith. The best time to do it is while all is calm and the sun is shining in your life. Waiting until the storm comes (or illness strikes) to build faith is like trying to lift a 100lbs weight, when you haven't successfully lifted 25lbs. Faith grows as we make it a part of our talk and our conversations.

The trying of our faith, of which James speaks about in the Bible, should happen long before we face the critical hour, when someone's life is on the line. That's no time to be "trying" anything. We should all be building our faith daily, just like we build our bodies with food and exercise. Start out small with something that is not a life or death predicament; I have used my faith to believe for a parking space at a crowded venue. I had a choice to either complain about the crowdedness, or to speak what I desired to the Lord. I chose to say, "Lord, please bless us with a good parking space. We thank you for it right now." Right then, as I approached our destination, a car started backing out, thus freeing up a space directly in front of the building. It has worked for me time after time. I heard another preacher say that he began by believing God for a pair of socks. You get the picture.

HOW WILL I KNOW MY FAITH IS BUILT UP?

Here are a few tips that will help you to know if your faith is growing. Since the definition of faith is the substance of things hoped for and the evidence of things not seen, you know your faith is developing when:

1. You believe you already own something you cannot see. You're not hoping it will come someday; you actually believe that you have it now.

2. You can stand on the Word, in spite of the contradictory symptoms your five senses are experiencing.

3. You have acquired patience (the quality that does not succumb to pressure nor bow to circumstances).

4. Time passing is no longer a reason to doubt, but to believe. You believe that each day is bringing you closer to the manifestation of your desire.

5. You simply will not take "no" for an answer.

Please be clear that this is about *you* building your own faith. When you bring others into the picture, especially believers, their level of faith must also be considered.

SECTION TWO

MY JOURNEY

I have no misconceptions about my role in the body of Christ. I am both a battle-tested veteran and a survivor. Having encountered years of long seesaw battles; seasons of nothing but waiting; and extended periods when difficult questions far outnumbered easy answers, I am certain of these two things: I know how to fight, and I know how to persevere.

At age 16, I became a believer and started this journey expecting—like the children of Israel—to forever leave behind the land of my bondage, and to enter into the exciting land God had promised. God said that it was a land that "flowed with milk and honey." I knew that for me, it would not be an actual physical place. I believed it to be an experience that eyes hadn't seen and ears hadn't heard. My expectations were to live a life in God's anointing, see his miracles daily, and prosper with power and victory.

Now, four decades later, the anticipation of crossing my Jordan is still strong and my enthusiasm, though tempered, has not waned. Like an anxious child, I am yet expecting what he promised. I must confess, I had no idea about all that would befall my life during the journey. What a colorful array it has been of revelations, challenges, victories, and experiences with God.

Anyone who has ever walked with him will agree: bad times with God are ultimately far better than the good times in the world. If you've studied the Bible, you've come to realize, as I have, that it's really not the destination, but the journey that is the most interesting. It was on the journey that the children of Israel walked through the sea on dry ground; ate "manna" from heaven; made bitter water sweet; received the 10 commandments, written by the hand of God; and learned the ways of God. I feel the same way about my life. I have learned many things "on the way" that are both eye opening and life changing. My role is to teach and share the knowledge I've learned, and skills I've acquired, with you.

CHAPTER FIVE

WAKE UP! SIN IS NOT YOUR PROBLEM

> *"...they which receive abundance of grace and of the gift of righteousness shall reign in life by one, Jesus Christ."*
> -Romans 5:17

> *"Awake to righteousness and sin not."* -I Corinthians 15:34

> *"For he hath made him to be sin for us, who knew no sin; that we might be made the righteousness of God in him."*
> -II Corinthians 5:21

Erroneous notions about what it means to be righteous are as out-of-place as weeds in a manicured lawn. Unfortunately, the Body of Christ is full of them. We take for granted that the meaning of righteousness is too obvious to research. Righteousness is commonly regarded as being in a state of perfection, or at least very near to it. It's one of those words that seems to explain itself.

"Right" implies the absence of, or departure from, wrong and wrongdoing. Therefore, a righteous man would be someone whose conduct is sinless. Because no one can perfectly fit that bill except Jesus, many have failed in the eyes of the world. Being "saved" has always meant being righteous, which also implied that sinning was a thing of the past. It's no wonder that high expectations have often been dashed when, upon close examination of the lives of believers, it was discovered that they routinely fell short of the goal of being sinless. No matter how long we have gotten the concept wrong, its proper meaning brings a wealth of knowledge, and authority, to those who will take the time to get it right.

RIGHTEOUSNESS IS A GIFT

Righteousness means being able to stand in God's presence without any sense of guilt, condemnation, or inferiority. This much sought after state-of-being, however, cannot be earned. So many have attempted but failed. To earn it would make it a reward for deeds done, trials endured, or feats accomplished. Relatively few individuals would then be able to obtain it.

Righteousness is a gift to all believers. Everyone loves to receive gifts, especially when they're unexpected and expensive. Righteousness fits both criteria. It was purchased with the precious blood of Jesus, and is quite an unexpected blessing to all. Also implied in the same verse, is that it leads to "reigning in life." That's right! Being right with God gives us the right to <u>rule on earth</u>. What could there be in righteousness that would qualify us to reign or rule in this life? It is right standing with God: a right relationship between us and Him.

Anyone who is right with God has already achieved the most sought after position there is in this life. What could be better? When we are right with God we have his favor, which causes us to be "more than conquerors through him that loved us."[22] This means that we who are striving to make it to heaven, don't have to wait to hear Jesus say, "Well done" to know that we are indeed righteous.

Man's original state was not a sinner. Adam was born (created) "right" with God. He received his righteous state from the beginning of his existence. He walked in right relationship with God, and began to take dominion just as God had commanded in Genesis 1:26. This was God's original design for man: to be born with righteousness intact. After Adam's fall, every human being was born in sin and separated from God at birth. Along with the fall came: guilt, shame, and condemnation—all were part of the curse. Jesus redeemed us from that curse when he sacrificed his life, so that we could be *born again* into righteousness with God. I have observed so many Christians who accept, as a fact, that we were born as sinners, but yet fail to accept that we can be born again into righteousness. If we accept the sin birth which resulted from Adam's wrong doing, we should much more willingly accept our righteous birth that resulted from Jesus' right doing. How can Adam's failure be more powerful than Jesus' success?

Many of the problems we face are not sin problems, but problems of not knowing our righteousness. The scripture in II Corinthians above calls us the righteousness of God. We were made to be that righteousness when Jesus was made to be sin for us. **It was the Great Exchange.** He took our sins and gave us his righteousness. We must embrace that wonderful reality. If we don't, we will dishonor the price he paid through his precious blood to return it (righteousness) to us. Say it: "I am the righteousness of God."

AWAKE TO RIGHTEOUSNESS

For years, ministers fell into the trap of preaching against sin, by spending a lot of time rebuking sinful actions: lying, stealing, committing adultery, fornicating, smoking, and drinking got top billing. The generations that were harangued by these caustic messages came away with more "sin consciousness" than "righteous consciousness." We once again wore the label "sinners, saved by grace," with the emphasis on "sinners." As a result, righteousness inherited a warped interpretation, and the righteous became the exclusive "members only" club of individuals who had conquered these vices. Only they could wear the white garments and instruct others. Pity on everyone else. To this day, it is generally accepted that right standing is earned by abstinence from the aforementioned vices. But as much as this gave preachers plenty of material, it misplaced the proper emphasis of right standing, and gave plenty of free advertisement to the work of the enemy.

The scripture states:[23] "Awake to righteousness and sin not." The implication is that we have been sleeping and need to wake up! Righteousness is something we need to wake up to; we must become aware that we already have it. It is a gift that we never dreamed we had. When we realize the wonderful favor and awesome power given us at birth, sin quickly becomes yesterday's news. I dare say sin is not the problem. Jesus took our sins away.[24] Being aware of our righteousness is the real challenge.

It's comical to see ministers and believers nervously tripping over themselves to maintain the appearance of being humble. Any compliment paid them is immediately brushed off with words that redirect the focus to someone else. Many are embarrassed to receive any honor at all. That may be the reason why the scriptures declare that God made us to be the righteousness of himself.[25] This is not left to our laboring. God already did it. Isaiah 54:17 states that our righteousness is of God. We must get used to being his righteousness. It doesn't mean that we're perfect right now or that we don't make mistakes. But the more we walk in this, the more we become like him. Jesus was made sin and we were made righteousness. Now we must learn to walk in the boldness of that fact.

Certain endeavors require boldness to achieve. We are encouraged, not to cower, but to come boldly to the precious throne of grace (unmerited favor) to find mercy and grace. Claiming our kinship as sons of God, driving out the powers of darkness, reclaiming our inheritance—all require right standing to achieve. Without knowing we are right with God, we will never attempt those feats. A vast ocean of blessing and accomplishments await the person who proceeds forth in right standing before God. But, the enemy has torpedoed many sea worthy vessels through guilt, condemnation and shame. These weapons have proved very effective in keeping us confined and in bondage to past failures, disappointments and mistakes. No one can wage effective warfare with this kind of baggage. Yet, all of us have experienced these self-defeating forces.

RIGHTEOUSNESS IS THE CURE

God is freely giving it as a gift to every believer. We must take time to get this concept into our spirits until it becomes like second nature to us. I believe that the Lord has been patiently waiting for his Body to receive his grace. What would it mean to actually realize that "I'm right with God!"? Practice it and experience its effects in your life.

WHEN WE SIN

What happens when we sin?—"If we confess our sins, he is faithful and just to forgive us our sins, and to cleanse us from all unrighteousness."[26]—Satan is no longer in charge of our sins. We are now God's children. When we sin, we don't run from, but *to* God. We confess our sins, then God takes over. He faithfully forgives us, and then he does something that is so wonderful: he cleanses us from **all** unrighteousness. When we are cleansed from **all** unrighteousness, it's like washing a stain out of our clothes. When a stained garment is clean, we're ready to wear it again. <u>We don't always feel righteous, but this is not a feeling—it's a truth.</u> As we speak his Word, in time, our feelings will get in line with the Word.

CHAPTER SIX

TRIALS DON'T COME TO MAKE YOU STRONG

"Let no man say when he is tempted, I am tempted of God: For God cannot be tempted with evil, neither tempteth he any man."
-James 1:13

"My brethren, count it all joy when ye fall into divers temptations; Knowing this, that the trying of your faith worketh patience."
-James 1:2-3

There is a commonly accepted misconception among believers that trials come only for the purpose of making us strong. It is repeated in our songs, sermons, and even in our daily conversations. However, much to the contrary, enduring trials without exercising faith can lead to serious loss. Trials alone don't make us strong. We need to make that distinction. Our opponent in the trial is not working for our good; rather, he is trying his best to destroy us. We all need to be aware of that. If not, we will fling open the doors of our lives and accept the "killing, stealing and destroying"[27] of the devil, as if it's an act of God.

Through this kind of thinking, God has gotten the blame for the tragic disasters that occur throughout the world. He's blamed for taking from his people the very money they need to survive, and for leaving them in lack. That's like saying storms, winds, and floods come to make our houses strong. On the contrary, our houses are not strong because of storms. They are strong in spite of them, because of how and where they are constructed. Trials alone are not working for us. **What makes us strong in the trial is our faith, and how we handle the Word of God in it.** We find that when we walk in faith, God consistently turns them around for our good, but that's not the intention for which they were sent.

This misconception permeates our gospel songs, and has been repeated as a proven fact for as far back as I can remember. This subtle message makes God both the sender of, and the deliverer from, the many trials that believers face every day. Our attitude toward trials has a lot to do with how we come out at the other end. We know that trials are inevitable. Therefore, we have developed the habit of accepting them as God-sent.

However, a closer look at the Word of God does not bear this out.

THE TRUE PURPOSE OF TRIALS

Trials, which many people think have come to make us strong, **are actually being sent with a more sinister intention. Through trials and temptations, the devil is planning to destroy your life.** Satan is not the teacher of the church. Neither is he employed by God to teach the church the ways of God. That would be like sending the fox to guard the chickens. If and when we fall into a trial or temptation, God will turn things around for our good. But he is not the tempter. "Let no man say when he is tempted, I am tempted of God: for God cannot be tempted with evil, neither tempteth he any man."[28]

It's not the trial alone, but it is the trying of our faith that is producing godly character.[29] It's what we do with our **faith** in the trial that means so much to our walk with God. Jesus, in Matthew 7:24, describes the storms that come into everyone's life by surmising that "he that heareth these sayings of mine and doeth them I will liken unto a man that built his house upon a rock." When the rains descended and the floods came and the wind blew and beat upon the house it didn't fall because the person was a doer of the Word; it's what we do in the storm that matters most. It's once again the trying of our faith in God's Word.

I believe that whenever the Word comes, deliverance comes. Ever vigilant, the enemy is desperate to erase it from our lives. Otherwise, the Word would accomplish its mission. The storm typifies the trials that come against us because of the Word. Notice that the storm was not trying to help the house remain standing. Unless built upon solid rock, the house will succumb to the destructive forces of the storm. We should also notice that the forces of destruction succeeded, where the Word was heard but not acted upon. Notice also the prayer of Jesus.[30] Jesus taught his disciples to pray, "And lead us not into temptation." If temptations, tests, and trials are good for us, why does he teach them to pray "lead us not into temptation"?

TRIAL'S DESTRUCTIVE FORCE

Trials alone don't increase faith. Otherwise, believers who have endured the most trials would be the strongest in faith. That's simply not the case. Instead, what we so often now witness is just the opposite. Many continue to live in defeat, even though they have endured many hardships along the way. Sickness and lack accompany far too many of our older, and more experienced, Christians.

Adam and Eve's trial did not make them stronger. When they both failed, it destroyed their perfect world, and plunged their descendants into the curse. If trials and tests make us strong, the Israelites in the wilderness should have been strengthened by theirs. Instead, their years in the wilderness hardened their hearts and eventually killed them. Almost the entire generation of Israelites who were delivered out of Egypt, died in the wilderness. In the New Testament, when Jesus was tempted in the wilderness, Satan was behind the attack—planning to destroy him if he made even one mistake. Rest assured, he was not there to strengthen Jesus in any way. Jesus said, "The thief comes only to steal, kill and destroy."[27] Apparently the only reason the enemy shows up is to perpetrate those crimes.

Further proof is found in 1 Corinthians 10:13 which states, *"There hath no temptation taken you but such as is common to man: but God is faithful, who will not suffer you to be tempted above that ye are able; but will with the temptation also make a way to escape, that ye may be able to bear it."* If temptation and tests are good for us, why does the Lord provide a way of escape? If it's helping us then why would there be a need for a way of escape?

CHAPTER SEVEN

TREAT SICKNESS LIKE YOU TREAT SIN

Bless the Lord O my soul and forget not all his benefits; Who forgiveth all thine iniquities and healeth all thy diseases.

-Psalm 103:2

When the evening was come, they brought unto him many that were possessed with devils; and he cast out the spirits with his word, and healed all that were sick. That it might be fulfilled which was spoken by the prophet Esaias the prophet, saying, Himself took our infirmities, and bare our sicknesses.

-Matthew 8:16-17

I was delighted to discover that healing is an integral part of the gospel. It's not merely a fringe benefit of salvation, but an essential component of it. Jesus went everywhere preaching the gospel and healing the sick. He even went so far as to raise from the dead those who got sick and died (e.g. Lazarus). Everywhere he went, he demonstrated that sickness would not be allowed to progress unchecked when he was there. The crowds expected it of him. People pressed in to touch even the hem of his garment, because it was known that healing—by the power of God—was present in his ministry. Nowadays, there are many who receive Christ as Savior, but never receive the healing that also belongs to them. For some reason, we readily receive the forgiveness of our sins, but not the release of our bodies from the physical penalty of that sin. Jesus told a man who was sick of palsy: "Be of good cheer your sins are forgiven." That man was not looking to hear that from the Savior; he just wanted to be healed. However, Jesus needed to get across to his followers the connection between sins forgiven and physical healing.

The principle is this: once sin is forgiven, or washed away from the soul of man, his body is judiciously released from the physical penalty. Throughout the Bible this pattern is repeated. Jesus was able to apply healing to the people of his time (seen in the scripture above from Matthew) because of his sacrifice that was soon to take place. Isaiah said that he (Jesus) took our infirmities and bore our sicknesses. I asked the Lord how he could heal sicknesses before the sacrifice was actually done. He said that in heaven, they count a thing in effect when it's spoken; that's when it becomes spiritual law. And spiritual laws govern and affect physical things, like your body. Time and time again, the pattern of atoning for sins, followed by release from physical confinement, was demonstrated.

Symbolically, the first Passover is a good example. Pharaoh had God's people in bondage and would not release them for weeks. That is, until the blood of the lamb was sprinkled over the doorposts and side posts. Once the blood of the innocent lamb was shed, the people were physically released from 400 years of bondage.

> *"He brought them forth also with silver and gold; and there was not one feeble person among them their tribes."*[31]

What a miracle! After centuries of slavery, to be released without one feeble person is the healing of an entire nation! The writer of Psalm 103 (mentioned above) repeats the pattern. He said, "Bless the Lord....forget not all his benefits. Who forgives all iniquities and heals all diseases." Once again, physical healing follows on the heels of forgiveness of sins. God did not save our souls, and leave our bodies to fend for themselves. His salvation is for the total man. His will is as definite to heal the body of sickness, as it is to heal the soul of sin. As stated above, Jesus essentially said to the sick of palsy: "cheer up because your sins are forgiven, which means that your healing is here as well."

Death came into the world because of sin. "Sickness is incipient death."[32] Sin can only be removed by the blood atonement of Jesus. But once sin is remitted and done away with, death loses its power over man in all its devious forms. Sickness has been defined as the foul offspring of its father Satan, and its mother sin. Once sin is washed away, sickness has no right to remain.

Another great symbol of this pattern is the brass serpent. The children of Israel had murmured and complained about the journey. As a result, poisonous snakes had come in and bitten the people, of which many died. When they cried out to God, he first forgave their sin. Then, Moses was instructed to make a brass serpent upon which if anyone looked, who had been bitten, would live. Once again, first the forgiveness of sins, then release from physical infirmity.

FALSELY ARRESTED

A friend of mine, Keith Moore, relayed a personal story to me that applies here. In his younger days, he got a traffic ticket, which he paid by the date it was due. To his surprise and alarm, he received a call from the police saying that there was a warrant for his arrest, for failure to pay. He assured them that payment was made, but they required him to come down to clear up the matter. He agreed to come on his way to work. Upon entering the police station, he was summarily arrested; stripped of his clothing; dressed in a prison jumpsuit; and thrown into a jail cell with 20 other prisoners. He argued to no avail that he had in fact paid the charges. They kept him in jail. Apparently, the money he had paid had not yet been recorded at the police station. The matter was cleared up when proof was given that the charges were paid. He went through this degrading ordeal because, although the charges were paid, the police didn't get the message.

Many people today remain physically incarcerated with sickness, because the message has not gotten through that all the charges have been dropped. No blessing of the kingdom comes without a fight. Your healing is a valuable commodity, well worth fighting for. The gospel we preach is that our sins are forgiven. Jesus paid it all. Now we must demand our freedom from our ancient jailor, Satan. He will try, but he cannot legally hold us in physical confinement.

All believers are aware that we no longer have to tolerate sin. It has no dominion over us. We don't have to lie, cheat, or steal. According to the Word of God, Jesus "bore our sins in his own body on the tree, that we being dead to sins should live unto righteousness, by whose stripes ye were healed."[33] If we don't have to live in sin—on the power of this scripture—it must also mean that we don't have to be sick. There's the pattern again. Don't treat sin one way, and sickness another. Treat sickness the same way you treat sin. Don't tolerate it, not for a moment.

SECTION THREE

ENTERING MY DARK PLACE

I entered into one trial that was so long, it was like walking through a dark unending cave. In 1994, I moved my family from Omaha to New York. I was taking a leap of faith into what I believed was the will of God for my life. Full time teaching ministry was my goal. I accepted preaching engagements, and started Bible study in my living room. We had moved into a rented home for a year, until our lease was up. Then, fortunately, I found an amazing opportunity: a house in the Hamptons, in foreclosure, that required approximately $8,500 to secure. "What a deal!" I thought. We would have our own house, at an amount I could afford, and I could begin enjoying some of the promised blessings of the Lord. Finally, I could see the light at the end of the tunnel. Little did I know, that light was the light of an oncoming train!

Because I had not been fully employed for more than a year, a traditional loan was out of the question. My hope was to get a trusted friend to advance me the money. That didn't happen. The reason was: "I have the money. But if I loan it to you, you will depend on me and not on God!" I didn't understand the logic, because I always depended on God. They knew that I was honest, and would not take advantage. Suddenly, we were without a place to live in New York. Essentially, we were now homeless.

My mother has always loved the fact that her son is in ministry. She has always bragged about me being a man of God. She volunteered for us to come and move in with her until we got on our feet. I drove around all week, frantically searching for a miracle to avoid this embarrassment. Finally, I had no other choice but to move in with her. To this very day, I cannot fully talk about how demeaning it was. It's yet too painful to accept. It was hard to face the facts of how low I had sunk. I have often held that my Father in heaven is rich. He owns a thousand houses, but his dedicated servant, Al Gee, for some reason was denied one. I had left my good paying job in government, to give my life to the work of the Lord. But there we were, the man of faith and his family, living with his mother. I don't think, even as of this writing, that I have fully recovered from that humiliation.

My predicament was so outrageously wrong. I could have and should have lost my mind! I could not explain to myself what was happening, let alone to my wife and children. I just got up the next day and simply… kept going. Each day, as I strained for any word from the Lord, that was the only statement I heard: "Just keep going!" I wondered out loud if I had somehow unwittingly committed sin and become the enemy of God. I remember screaming at God in utter distress, "I must be your enemy because I know you don't treat your friends like this!" Though surrounded by family, I was so alone with what I believed. I had few results to rely upon. It was a lonely place: like a solitary confinement.

I have gladly taught prosperity to God's people, because I'm convinced it's part of the gospel. So, it was a trial to watch as others prospered, while I waited on the Lord. There were those preachers who didn't preach the same word of faith I did, but they met me at the airport in their luxury cars and drove me to their fine homes. They ate at the finest restaurants, while I could only afford a cramped rented space, and a used car. My trials have been long and hard. And everything I've gotten worth anything, has come with a fight. Everything!

CHAPTER EIGHT

THE FAULT OF FINDING FAULT

(A Critical Spirit)

"Do all things without grumbling and faultfinding and complaining (against God) and questioning and doubting (among yourselves)..."
-Philippians 2:14 Amplified

"Neither murmur ye, as some of them also murmured and were destroyed of the destroyer."
-I Corinthians 10:10

A child of God who has a critical spirit can always see the flaws in a program, project, or person. He or she can be critical of anything and everything. This person finds faults and complains habitually. Being a carrier of this spirit can be tragic for anyone. The individual inevitably ends up being in trouble with God. An entire generation of people perished in the wilderness for this very same thing. The children of Israel found out the hard way that being critical can make you ineligible for God's blessings. I think we all agree that constructive criticism is valuable to the success of any program. Scrutinizing individual and corporate performance is very useful for future improvements and success. But a critical spirit is not constructive; it's just the opposite. It discourages those who are striving to follow God's vision, and hinders every attempt at unity.

The Israelites found out that God's people don't have the prerogative to murmur and complain. Especially when their daily provisions are being provided by the very hand of God. Murmuring is a useless exercise. It takes precious time away from praising and expressing thanks to the Lord—who does everything well. Murmuring implies that somehow God has mistakenly forgotten some detail that's important to the well-being of his people. The Jews murmured when they crossed the Red Sea, and found the water bitter on the other side. When God remedied that situation, they murmured about the road they were traveling, and about the food God had provided, and ultimately, about the very land God had promised them. No one, not even God himself, can satisfy a person who has a critical spirit. He could not give them his best, even though that was his plan to do so all along. God's best requires trusting him—i.e. faith. After much patience with his murmuring people, God sternly commanded them to turn back into the wilderness. Since they constantly complained, he waited decades until they all died, then offered the same blessing to their children.

The critical spirit refuses to trust God, and only sees the physical circumstances. As the old song says: circumstances are "sometimes up, sometimes down, and sometimes level to the ground." Riding the roller coaster of circumstances was never God's intended lifestyle for his people. He said, "Thou shalt be above only and thou shalt not be beneath."[34] Outward circumstances change often, and are unreliable indicators of God's blessing. He said, "Trust in the Lord with all thine heart and lean not unto thine own understanding. In all thy ways acknowledge him and he shall direct thy path."[35] Though we are all tempted to complain about our present situation, to do so may immediately stop the blessings. We are better served by meditating on the goodness of God. There is always something good to think on with God. And no matter what you are experiencing, there's always someone who is in a much worse predicament.

CHAPTER NINE

STRIFE: SATAN'S PERFECT SPOILER

"For where envying and strife is, there is confusion and every evil work."

-James 3:16

I believe strife is a spirit, that is the root cause of a countless number of relationships gone sour. Relationships in families, marriages, businesses, and even ministries—all have been the prey of the spirit of strife. History is littered with the charred remains of relationships that began in sweet peace and love, only to be destroyed by it. Strife is a much too effective weapon of the enemy, because if left to work over a period of time, it destroys from the inside out. From the ancient conflict between Cain and Able, to the present day conflicts among the nations, strife is the culprit. It is Satan's perfect spoiler.

Strife in the Amplified Bible is defined as contention, rivalry, and selfish ambition. It cannot be allowed free reign in any serious ministry, or relationship. Jesus said, "A house divided against itself cannot stand." Envying and strife not only cause conflict, but they open the door to "every evil work." It is to be avoided like the plague.

DON'T LET THE SUN GO DOWN ON STRIFE

Paul admonished the church at Ephesus: [36] "Be ye angry and sin not; let not the sun go down upon your wrath; Neither give place to the devil." Experienced believers who are married know that it's a mistake to allow anger to fester overnight without reconciling. The enemy takes advantage, and uses the whole night to deepen his hold, and intensify the contention. When the morning comes, strife picks up where it ended, with a night's worth of ill feelings that have festered within. Couples stop speaking, and begin avoiding each other. From that point, the situation deteriorates, falling prey to strife's wicked strategy.

Ministries that allow strife to continue unaddressed, and unexposed, do so to their own demise. Naïve, but well-intentioned, leaders have learned by trial and error that "goats" cannot be given the same treatment as "sheep." Sheep have no problem following the shepherd, goats do. Sheep are submissive and trainable. However, goats are rebellious and stubborn. Goats characteristically butt against plans and programs they don't like. Not wanting to confront those who are contentious, or outright rebellious, plays into the hands of the enemy. Strife will not relent from its destructive agenda if allowed to continue.

Failure to confront its carriers is a grave error. It knows no compromise. If not exposed and expelled, unity and harmony will become memories. The numerous ministry breakups and separations we have today are all testimony to its damaging effects. The counsel of the Holy Spirit will be crucial here as to the proper approach, when the problem must be addressed. But ultimately, we must keep the vigil Paul admonished, and commit to "giving no place to the devil."

ABSALOM: SON OF STRIFE

Because of his love for his son Absalom, David allowed him to stand before the people and openly criticize his performance as king. David was obviously blinded by love. He was unable or unwilling to see the hate his son harbored in his heart against him, and its potential danger. Absalom took advantage of that love by presenting himself to the people as a better ruler than his father. His every move was a calculated conspiracy against King David. An experienced ruler like David should have immediately removed Absalom from any influence over the people. This would have cut strife off at the root. Instead he allowed it to continue. Over time, Absalom stole the hearts of the people, and when the opportunity presented itself, launched a coup to dethrone his own father. His devious plan was so well coordinated, that by the time David was alerted, the forces of Absalom were taking over the kingdom. David had to hastily gather his belongings to escape with his life. The force of strife had done its damage. The entire kingdom was now in danger. Fortunately, in the ensuing battle, David's forces defeated the army of Absalom. Absalom was also killed. When David heard the news of his son's death, he wept bitterly in complete knowledge that was obvious to his subjects; he had permitted his son to foment strife that nearly destroyed Israel.[37]

Seeds of strife must never be allowed to grow. Both love and wisdom will be required for its expulsion. If left to its devices, it will always produce the bitter fruit of destruction. It is the destroyer of kingdoms and homes alike. Jesus said, "Any kingdom filled with civil war is doomed, so is a home filled with argument and strife."[38]

CHAPTER TEN

PROCRASTINATION: THE SILENT DESTROYER

Then Pharaoh called for Moses and Aaron and said, "Entreat the Lord, that he may take away the frogs from me, and from my people; and I will let the people go, that they may do sacrifice unto the Lord. And Moses said unto Pharaoh, "Glory over me: when shall I entreat for thee, and for thy servants, and for the people, to destroy the frogs from thee and thy houses, that they may remain in the river only: "And he said, "Tomorrow"

-Exodus 8:8-10

And he said unto another, Follow me. But he said, Lord, suffer me first to go and bury my father. Jesus said unto him, "Let the dead bury their dead: but go thou and preach the kingdom of God. And another also said, Lord, I will follow thee; but let me first go bid them farewell, which are at home at my house. And Jesus said unto him, "No man, having put his hand to the plow, and looking back, is fit for the kingdom of God.

-Luke 9:59-62

If there is any more subtle a destroyer of lives, ministries, and dreams, than procrastination, I don't know it. Here is an unseen foe straight from the hand-picked ranks of the enemy, hiding under cover in people's attitudes and habits, deadly in its effect. This one thing derails more well-meaning people than anything I have ever encountered. Procrastination is silent and subtle, but deadly.

The first account mentioned above, is that of Pharaoh who, when asked when he wanted God to remove the plague of frogs, answered: "Tomorrow." Why tomorrow? Why not today? Especially since this is God who is performing the miracle. This is so indicative even of God's people who have the same attitude. We are living for God who is the very best of the best. Walking in the better covenant with better promises, but putting off for tomorrow, what should be accomplished today.

LOOKING FOR THE RAPTURE

Too often, we relegate for tomorrow what should be taken, and claimed, today. I think the misconception lies in the fact that our hope rested in a much talked about future event called the rapture. *"Then we which are alive and remain shall be caught up together with them in the clouds, to meet the Lord in the air..."* (I Thes.4:17). This was the message so fervently delivered to my generation (baby boomers). All eyes for a time were pointed heavenward, looking for the soon return of the Lord. Years ago, we expected that Jesus was coming so soon, we didn't dare venture into any place that we thought might displease him. We feared he might come and "catch us with our work undone." Some even put future plans on hold, fully expecting that we were in the very last hours of time. The air was full of expectancy of his imminent return. Some decades later, we still have the expectancy, but we have found that before we go to heaven, we must exercise our God-given authority here. Putting everything on hold for tomorrow was a mistake. Back then, we read in the scriptures that the world would get worse and worse. All hope for improvements in the society, and the world at large, were done away with. We had made it into the ark of safety, and were now waiting for the ride out of here. Such a focus on tomorrow was consuming all of our precious todays.

Everything with God is now. He exists in the present moment at all times. Faith is now. Every moment is a now moment. We don't live in tomorrow; only in the "right now." For that reason, it's critical to our spiritual well-being to get the things done that God has placed on our hearts—now. Jesus said, "Take no thought for tomorrow." (Matt. 6:34) That doesn't mean we don't plan, but rather that we don't worry about tomorrow.

We all have a tendency to put things off that seem unpleasant or laborious. Jesus let his disciples know, from the beginning, that there was no greater work or event, than what he was doing, and that delay was not an option.

He is the way; the truth; and the life; and the only way to the Father (John 8:32). All priorities must bow to his work in the earth. The business of saving and reconciling mankind to God is the top priority. We are used to having choices and options, but when Jesus came with the long awaited salvation and deliverance, there was no longer any legitimate reason for procrastination. We must get on with the work.

When God speaks to us, we must hang on every word. Whether his message comes through others or directly from him, it is God speaking. I've noticed that there are people who, after hearing a message that "hits home" in their hearts, immediately begin to take action. Then there are those who hear a great message, respond emotionally, but never act on what was said. The very next week, they return to get another emotional experience. The former grow and reach the next level in God; the latter remain stuck and eventually become stagnant.

Anyone plagued by procrastination is bound to live a life that will end in regret, of what should have or could have been.

CHAPTER ELEVEN

NEGLECT: THE THIEF OF FUTURE BLESSINGS

"...For unto whomsoever much is given, of him shall be much required:"

-Luke 12:48

Some leaders suffer from a malady that totally disqualifies them from leadership. They have a problem making tough decisions because of a crippling need to be liked. For those who lead, neglecting to make tough decisions immediately disqualifies them from the leadership role. God is a God of order. He has done all that was needed to set things up for his children.[39] Now he needs a decision. He is set to respond upon an informed decision. Things must be in proper order before he will release his provisions. Until the proper order is demonstrated, the blessings which belong to us will be held up. **Leaders must either make tough unpopular decisions, or get out of the way of those who will.**

God does not spare those who love him, and who are in leadership, from completing unpleasant tasks. His love does not look away when this basic duty is neglected. God's grace does not stop when leaders abandon basic laws of conduct and order. Likewise, it also cannot protect them from the consequences of that neglect. As a matter of fact, because of their positions, expectations on them are much greater than on those who follow their lead. Because of the influence every leader has on others, their decisions, or lack thereof, affect the future and direction of many.

God never wanted Israel to have a king. He told them so through the prophet Samuel.[40] But they wanted to be like other nations. He knew that the leadership of fallible men would lead them away from the covenant with Him, and it did. It was the leadership that caused Israel to suffer plagues of disease, and utter defeat on the battlefield. The leadership caused them to follow strange gods, and to commit idolatry. Leadership caused them to be driven out of the very land God gave them. For instead of making the tough decisions needed for sound structure, their leaders failed.

In the Old Testament,[41] the priest Eli neglected to stop his sons from defiling the priesthood with fornication and thievery. He operated well in the office of the priesthood, but made little effort to control his sons who had the outrageous audacity to work wickedness, as priests before the Lord. God did not immediately judge his actions, but in time, the hammer of judgment fell. Eli's entire male offspring died in one day, including his unborn grandson. This destruction was all because of Eli's neglect of leadership responsibilities—as a father and as a high priest. The lesson to be learned here is that although we are given leadership positions which allow us to influence others, the position itself is not a license to stray from the sound principles. Parents must discipline their children early and continuously. People must know where we stand on important issues in the home. Debts should be paid in a timely fashion, and, our word should be our bond. Breaking basic laws of integrity will backfire, and cause heartache and embarrassment.

Paul gave good principles for leadership to follow: he said, *"add to your faith, virtue and to virtue knowledge, and to knowledge temperance, and to temperance patience, and to patience godliness, and to godliness brotherly kindness, and to brotherly kindness charity."* He stated, *"if ye do these things, ye shall never fall."*[42]

CHAPTER TWELVE

BE BITTER OR GET BETTER

If one lesson has hit home from the experience of the Israelites, it is: "don't allow the hard things you've experienced to harden your spirit against God." Some who endure hard tests and trials display a telltale hardness of spirit: a bitterness and cynicism from years of battle and hardship. When they talk of their experiences with God, and his promises, a stale air of doubt is present. It's as if their experiences have taught them to live according to the word of God, but to expect very little. "After all," they caution, "you don't want to be disappointed"; while others, who endure hard trials and tests, seem to increase in a sweet childlike trust in the Lord, maintaining an air of excitement every day. What's the difference between the two? The latter has not allowed the trials to harden their heart.

KEEP YOUR HEART

The heart of man, I believe, is his spirit. It's what the scriptures call the "inner man" or the "hidden man."[43] It's the center of our being. It's also a very important place to God. That's where God communicates with man. Proverbs 20:27 states: "The spirit of man is the candle of the Lord." Without access to the heart of man, God is limited in what he can reveal to him. The heart or spirit of man is the key area of God's dealings with man. It's no mystery why the enemy works through the difficult trials to cause a hardness, or a resistance in that area, to the things of God.

Proverbs 4:23 states: *"Keep your heart with all diligence for out of it flows the issues of life."* All of God's most meaningful work is done there. We must therefore take care to keep our spirit open and pliable to God, keeping out anything that would cause resistance to the Lord. This is where the seed of the Word of God is planted and germinated for the expected 30, 60, and 100 fold harvest. It must be ready at all times to receive the Word of God, no matter how farfetched the task that God wants us to accomplish.

For some of us, our trials have been long in duration, and time between conflicts has been short. This provides a fitting pretext for allowing discouragement to enter. Because our "due season" has been long in coming, we allow our confidence in the Word of God to wane. This is the time to be very watchful. When the manifestation of the things we are believing God for has not yet materialized, and we have been standing for a long time, any casual observer would agree that we now have the right to be battle weary. But those who know the things of God, know that it's not our strength we are relying on.

ELIJAH'S RETREAT

Elijah succumbed to this type of pressure when Jezebel threatened him.[44] When the report reached her that Elijah had not only exposed her false god, but had also had them killed, she swore to kill him. Totally disregarding the fact that he had just taken part in one of the greatest demonstrations of the power of God ever recorded (he had literally prayed fire down from heaven), fear caused him to run for his life. His thinking became completely irrational. Ostensibly, to escape death he ran from Jezebel. Yet when he prayed, he asked God to take his life. Without hesitation, Jezebel would have gladly accommodated his request. In order to get him into a position to listen, the Lord gave him food and water for strength, and after Elijah rested, God was able to get a word in. He asked him, "What are you doing here?" Fear had seized his heart and Elijah was far off course. He had allowed himself to descend into fear and self-pity. He said to the Lord, "I'm the only prophet left and now they're seeking to kill me." God had to bring Elijah back to his senses by giving him instructions on his next assignment, and also by letting him in on a secret. The secret was that God had in reserve seven thousand more individuals who could fill the prophet's shoes. His misguided fear and dramatic display of concern for saving God's "last prophet" was almost laughable.

THE REMEDY FOR HARDNESS OF HEART

Paul and Silas gave us the cure for hardness caused by hard trials.[45] After performing a great miracle by casting out an evil spirit, they were rewarded by being severely beaten, and thrown into jail. Jail in ancient times wasn't, by any stretch of the imagination, a place anyone wanted to be. There they were, minsters of the Most High God, locked behind bars. Having been stripped, beaten, and publicly humiliated, the two could have been more than a little perturbed that the almighty God allowed this to happen to them. Instead, they openly prayed and sang praises unto God. That must have been quite a shock to the devil. He had done his best to evoke anguish in their spirits, and doubts in their minds. But they wisely resisted the temptation to be hardened against God. This was truly a good opportunity to wonder, "Where is God, and what is he doing?" They both openly prayed and sang praises unto God. Praises in the midst of hardship, and in the face of seeming defeat, have reversed many downhill catastrophes, and transformed them into victories. Unknown to Paul and Silas, God was using this predicament as a means to save the jailor and his family, and to establish the new church at Philippi.

Praises are devastating to the enemy, but empowering to the believer.[46] If done in earnest, praises have a refreshing, uplifting, and delivering effect on man's spirit. God inhabits the praises of his people. Hardness cannot remain in the person who will open himself to give God praise.

In our lives, there will be many opportunities to be disappointed with the outcomes of certain situations. God gets the blame much too often. The temptation is to be angry with him, and to allow bitterness to harden our hearts against him. Don't fall for this strategy. Beside God, there is no one who loves us nearly as much. He has proven his love over and over again. Whenever tempted to be critical of the way God is operating, remember the verse in Romans 8:32 that states: "He that spared not his own Son, but delivered him up for us all." I have resolved that "until I'm ready to offer my son, I cannot dare question the motives of the one who did." This calms disappointment and softens our approach, allowing us to patiently wait until the Lord accomplishes his will in us.

SECTION FOUR

MY CONSOLATION

My consolation in all of my experiences has been something that God revealed to me. He said that there are two categories of spiritual leaders. One that demonstrates right now the manifestation of the Word spoken years ago, like Jesus and the disciples. At the proper time, they acted on the Word and results followed. They did miracles in line with the words God spoke through his prophets years prior. The second group, is people who have the task of doing something for which there are no prior references, like Abraham and Noah. No one had had a child from a promise at one hundred before Abraham came on the scene. And, no one had seen the rain like happened in the time of Noah. But these two pioneers had to withstand decades of waiting, while at the same time others were living their lives in normal fashion. Both these leaders had to endure. Noah had to endure 100 years of the jeers of generations of people, as he obediently constructed an ocean liner on dry land. Likewise, Abraham had to endure the scornful laughter of everyone who heard his name called the "father of many nations," while he and Sarah suffered decades of going without their own child. They both endured, to be able to create with God something new. For Abraham, it was a child at 100 years old. For Noah, it was rain that would not stop for 40 days and nights. It took long days and hours of waiting to bring these things to pass, but they came to pass.

I believe that I am involved in setting up the groundwork of bringing a season to pass, that eyes have not seen, and ears have not heard. Please don't think for a minute that I am on some ego trip. The years of waiting have taken any chance of that happening totally out of the realm of possibilities. I just believe God, and that he will fulfill his word to me. My great consolation for all the waiting and lack of results is that I am in good company. Noah, Abraham, Joseph, Joshua, Moses, etc.—all had to endure the season of lack of results while God fashioned something new. I am excited, because I know God can take one year and make up for all the years that have passed. If he is anything, he is faithful.

CHAPTER THIRTEEN

HOW CAN I HEAR THE VOICE OF GOD?

I must confess some frustration with God from time to time. Of course it was self-inflicted frustration, caused mainly by my ignorance. My frustration was that whenever I cried out to God, I would get silence. Even in times when a decision had to be made, I'd cry out to him and listen for his response; again all I would get was an empty silence. After a few times doing this, my frustration yielded to alarm. It was shocking that someone who has walked with God for the years I have, could not get a response from the Lord.

I wondered, how can I hear his voice? I was really in a predicament. I had his Word which states, "The Lord hear thee in the day of trouble; the name of the God of Jacob defend thee; Send thee help from the sanctuary, and strengthen thee out of Zion."[46] But though the Word was reassuring, it didn't satisfy my need. When I left the issue alone for a while, I could sense the Lord urging me to dig a little more: deeply with the Word and with books he had me to read. I was not surprised to learn that God was speaking all the time, but I was tuned in to the wrong frequency. There's a way God speaks to his people that is his preferred mode of communication: it is by the Spirit.

Proverbs 20:27 gives some insight: "The spirit of man is the candle of the Lord." Since we no longer use candles in the same way people in the Bible days did, we would say, "The spirit of man is the light bulb of the Lord." In other words, this implies that God communicates mainly with the spirit of man. He communicates with us in our inner man. This is center or the heart of man; a part in each of us that is higher than both the natural intellect and physical feelings. This is the spirit of man. *God is a spirit.*[48] He reveals things to us, and talks to us from his spirit directly into our spirit.

How is this done? By revelation, which is God illuminating certain things to us by his spirit. The Bible words it this way, *"As it is written, Eye hath not seen, nor ear heard, neither have entered into the heart of man, the things which God hath prepared for them that love him. But God hath revealed them unto us by his Spirit: for the Spirit searches all things, yea, the deep things of God."* [49]

THE AGE OF BEING LED BY THE SPIRIT

This is the age of the leading of the Holy Spirit. Placed here by God to train all newborn believers in the ways of the spirit, the Holy Spirit teaches us all things. He is called the Spirit of Truth. We cannot afford to be out of step with his methods or his manner. Just as when Jesus was on earth, he was the main focus. So now the Holy Spirit is the present manifestation of God in the earth. The whole thing is his project. We must cooperate with him in order to get anything from the Lord.

This is different, unfamiliar, and even strange to some, but Paul said, "as many as are led by the Spirit they are the sons of God." [50] He said, "the spirit bears witness with our spirit that we are the children of God." [51] He also assured everyone that there can be no condemnation to those in Christ, who walk after the Spirit and not the flesh (or the natural senses).[52] Our natural minds, with natural intellect, attempt to do what is natural to us. The Lord is taking the foolish things of this world to confound the wise.[53] Natural intelligence cannot take the lead on this one; it was never meant to take the lead. Only when man fell from grace, did the natural intellect become prominent. But from the beginning, man was designed to be like his father—God.

WAYS GOD SPEAKS TO US

How do we communicate with God if he is not connected to our natural minds? By what mode of communication can we speak with him?

I Corinthians 14:2 states: *"he that speaketh in an unknown tongue speaketh not unto men, but unto God. For no man understandeth him; howbeit in the spirit he speaketh mysteries."* This is now God's chosen form of direct communication. Beyond the natural senses and natural intellect, we communicate with God spirit to spirit. The language of the spirit has come into prominence. There is no longer any delay in receiving from God. We can receive as little, or as much, as we desire. Praying in this language provides an intimate connection with God.

God will also speak to you indirectly through other means, such as a song touching your deepest need with the words and music. Some people have dreams, in which God gives a much needed answer or direction. Additionally, how many times has God spoken directly to your hearts by an anointed message from his Word?

There are also those times when God will give you a message through nature: a modern day parable using something in the natural to explain a deep spiritual truth. For example, Jesus started a message with the words: "A sower went forth to sow." [54] I have even known him to use "trying" circumstances to get across a message, without the use of words. He may not speak in a language we can detect, but when he speaks, we receive a "knowing" or intuition in our spirit. Some have described the experience of communicating with God like becoming pregnant. When we leave an interaction with him, there's now something living inside of us.

Hebrews 8:10 states that God will write his laws in our hearts. His message is delivered into our hearts like the mail carrier delivering the mail. We have to go to the mailbox and get it. Jesus said, *"my sheep hear my voice."*[55] Practice believing his word by saying, "I know his voice. I hear his voice. I promptly and quickly obey."

KNOWING

Knowing from this time on is no longer an exercise of the mind alone, but a condition of the spirit. Knowledge is now downloaded from him to us, and we are not limited by what the mind cannot grasp. In time, the mind begins to understand what the spirit already knows. After praying this way, our inner man—or spirit—gets a message of peace calming our whole being, while the mind is still grappling with the problem.

Sadly though, if we neglect to spend time praying in the spirit and meditating on his word, there will be a noticeable lack of direction and counsel from God. Huge gaps in our counsel from the Lord can often be the result of a lack of communication with him in this manner. According to Isaiah 29:11-12, "With stammering lips and another tongue will he speak to this people. This is the rest wherewith ye may cause the weary to rest and this is the refreshing."

In literally every situation we face, there is a part we handle, and a part to be handled by God. Doing our part diligently is admirable, as long as we don't stop there. God has a part. Everything has a spiritual element, even if it's not readily noticeable. Proverbs 3:5-6 states, *"Trust in the Lord with all thine heart and lean not unto thine own understanding. In all thy ways acknowledge him and he shall direct thy path"*. There is a God-ward and a man-ward side to everything. Psalm 127:1 reads: *"Except the Lord build the house, they labor in vain that build it; except the Lord keep the city, the watchman waketh but in vain."* Let us not ignore the God-ward side.

This is the voice from heaven with the view from heaven that we can access anytime we wish. Access it! James said, *"If any man lack wisdom let him ask of God who gives liberally to every man."* [56]

As believers, let us quickly grow out of the need for outward signs to communicate with God. Let the outward signs be for the unbeliever. He has an inward way to communicate with us. A way neither the devil, nor our own intellect, can tamper with. It's called being led by the Spirit.

AVOIDING DISASTER

In my travels, I remember so vividly an incident that confirmed the wonderful privilege I have experienced by praying in the spirit. In the airport in Chicago, I had just walked down the platform, entered the plane, and found my seat. I was one of the first people to board, which gave me time to adjust my seat and get comfortable for the flight home. Nothing seemed out of the ordinary; just a typical flight on a typical day.

Suddenly, in my spirit, I felt the urging to pray in the spirit as rapidly as I could manage. It was urgent and unusually forceful (Those who pray often know that the Spirit is gentle and not usually a driving force). I complied, and quietly prayed, wondering what was going on behind the scenes. I prayed until the Spirit's urgency subsided. Then, over the speaker, came the voice of the pilot. "We have found a problem with the plane and will have to be here a while until the problem is repaired." I thanked God for having me pray. I believe that prayer was for the sole purpose of avoiding a disaster in the making. Since that time, I have always trained my spirit to be sensitive to the urging of the Holy Spirit.

Having direct communication with Him is a priceless benefit.

CHAPTER FOURTEEN

HEARING IS NOT ENOUGH

"So then faith cometh by hearing, and hearing by the word of God."
                                                              -Romans 10:17

"For unto us was the gospel preached, as well as unto them but the word preached did not profit them, not being mixed with faith in them that heard it."
                                                              -Hebrews 4:2

Years ago, the revelation came about how to increase faith, and it was a welcomed remedy. Up to that point, we prayed and hoped the prayer would come to pass. If we needed faith, we simply asked God for more. We were unaware that God had already placed into our hands the way to increase our own faith: by hearing the word of God.

When it was learned that, according to the scripture, it came by consistently, and routinely, hearing the word of God, hearing the word became the main focus. There was a hunger to feed on as much as could be consumed. Sermons, teaching tapes, books, etc. were devoured like faith food.

And as the word was heard, we sensed the strengthening of faith. At that time, it was mistakenly assumed that things would begin to change as faith was increased, but that did not automatically occur. Why not? **Because hearing the word in itself only increases your capacity for faith.** The actions that are taken when the word is meditated on, and consumed, completes the process.

Many individuals jumped on the faith bandwagon: confessing, hearing and declaring. "Name it and claim it" was the term that labeled this zealous group. But when results did not come right away, people were offended. This caused some people to get discouraged, and to conclude that it just doesn't work. Faith is not merely what you hear, but what you do with what you hear. After we load up on the word of God—whatever form that takes—it's time to act. **It's not only knowing the truth, but acting on the truth that is faith.**

MIX THE WORD WITH FAITH ACTION

In the scripture above, in Hebrews, Paul writes that this gospel—or good news—was preached to us the same as it was delivered to the Israelites. But, Paul went on to say, *"the word preached did not profit them, not being mixed with faith in them that heard it."*[57] It was great news to be promised your own land after having been so long in slavery, in Egypt. Likewise, it's great news to be promised healing; prosperity; and unconditional love; when for so long we have experienced the opposite.

In the book of Acts, chapter 14:8-9 reads: *"And there sat a certain man at Lystra, impotent in his feet, being a cripple from his mother's womb, who never had walked; The same heard Paul speak: who stedfastly beholding him, and perceiving that he had faith to be healed, Said with a loud voice, "Stand upright on thy feet, And he leaped and walked."* Hearing the word, as in this case, did something on the inside of this man, but faith or an action had to be mixed with that word.

FAITH: YOUR WORKING SERVANT

When asked by the disciples to increase their faith,[58] Jesus said if you have faith the size of a mustard seed, you can speak to a sycamine tree and it would obey you. But then, he spoke of having a servant who, after working in the field, is expected to continue to work in the house, to do whatever is needed to be done there as well. Faith is our servant, and it is to be exercised to serve in every area of need. The just shall live by faith.[59]

In God's blessing plan for Israel,[60] the Lord promised to command the blessing in *"All that thou settest thine hand unto."* This speaks of God's promised blessing upon every project they not only planned, but started to accomplish. Likewise, David wrote: *"Whatsoever he doeth shall prosper"* as the statement of promise given in Psalms 1:3. Apparently, even meditation practiced day and night in the Word is powerless to produce in the absence of doing. Jesus said, *"Whosoever heareth these sayings of mine and doeth them, I will liken unto a wise man which built his house upon a rock..."* [61] Hearing the words of Jesus is a great privilege. Doing them is an even greater one.

CHAPTER FIFTEEN

WAVERING DISQUALIFIES YOUR PRAYER

> "But let him ask in faith, nothing wavering. For he that wavereth is like a wave of the sea driven with the wind and tossed. For let not that man think that he shall receive any thing of the Lord."
>
> -James 1:6-7

What a thief wavering is! It immediately disqualifies us from receiving anything from the Lord. This is a very sobering reality. It partly explains the widespread lack of answered prayers among the Body of Christ today. The seriousness of this obstacle is enough to make us check each prayer to make sure we have rid ourselves of it. Whatever natural inclination we have toward it must be discovered and corrected. We cannot afford to carry this with us any longer.

In the Amplified Bible, the word "wavering" is defined as hesitating and doubting. What the Bible is saying here is: when you ask, there should be no hesitating and no doubting. If there is wavering, we will fail to receive, not only what we're presently praying for, but everything we pray for will be affected.

Faith requires that we take a stand, and not back up. In order for God to move on our behalf, some matters require certainty. Wavering destroys that element. It displays an inherent distrust of God and his Word. The faith stand must be on solid ground. And what is more solid than the Word of God? In Mark 11:24, Jesus said, "...When you pray, believe that you receive, and you shall have it." <u>This small phrase is often the most critical, but most neglected part of the prayer.</u>

We must then of necessity make certain our requests are based on the Word of God. Make sure that what we are asking is in the will of God. Healing, for example, is God's will. Because Jesus said in Mark 16:18, *"...they shall lay hands on the sick, and they shall recover,"* and "with his stripes we are healed."[62] Prosperity is the will of God for his people, as recorded in III John 1:2 *"Beloved, I wish above all things that thou mayest prosper and be in health, even as thy soul prospereth."* We can take a stand when praying for things along this line. For we are not only praying what we desire, but we have found that we are praying what God wants. Surely he will bring to pass what he wants, if we take a stand in agreement with him. Knowing God's will on the subject is half the battle. Therefore, we have taken the time to make sure it's in God's will. This increases our confidence of success.

John wrote: "And this is the confidence that we have in him, that if we ask any thing according to his will, he heareth us: *And if we know that he hear us, whatsoever we ask, we know that we have the petitions that we desired of him."* [63]

When we pray, we must be specific and resolute. Jesus was resolute when he said, *"Everyone that asks receives."*[64] Failure in this area of our lives is not an acceptable option.

CHAPTER SIXTEEN

WHY ARE YOU ASKING FOR WHAT'S ALREADY YOURS?

Although we often say the opposite, many of us are overly dependent upon our physical senses. Unless we see something happen with our natural eyes, we really don't believe it. A prime example is the way we misuse the word "bless" in our prayers. It's thrown around like someone waving a magic wand, touching each person with its magical powers. What do we mean when we pray saying, "Lord, please bless Mr. Brown"? Ephesians 1:3 states that *God has blessed us with all spiritual blessings* in the heavenly places in Christ. II Peter 1:3 states that *God has given us all things that pertain to life and godliness.* Why are we praying for what **has already been given?** And how does God answer this prayer? And what would be the proof that he has answered it, when we ask him to "bless" a particular person? To which of the thousands of blessings are we referring? Would God be obligated to do anything more than he has already done to satisfy that request? We must acknowledge what God has already done in our praying, and give him thanks. The time we spend in prayer this way can really be wasted time, if we are not being more specific about what we desire, and more aware of what God has already done.

Healing for our physical bodies falls into a similar dilemma. Matthew 8:17 states: *"Himself **took our infirmities**, and **bore our sicknesses**."* And I Peter 2:24 states: "...by whose stripes ye were healed." These scriptures place healing for our physical bodies into the past. Jesus purchased it long ago when he died on the cross. We are not trying to get healed. **WE ARE HEALED, AND THE ENEMY IS ATTEMPTING TO STEAL IT FROM US.**

We see the same pattern when God dealt with Israel regarding the conquest of the Promised Land. God said to Joshua, *"Every place that the sole of your foot shall tread upon, **that have I given unto you.**"*[65] To God, the Promised Land was already theirs for the taking. To those who didn't believe him, it was a different story altogether. They said, *"We be not able to go up against the people; for they are stronger than we."*[66] Because of this evil statement uttered in direct contradiction to what God said, they were disqualified from ever entering the land God promised. Instead, they were forced to return back to the wilderness. God was grieved with them because, after walking with him for so many years, they still didn't know his way of doing things. **He finishes a work, then invites mankind to believe and appropriate it for his own life.** Because the Israelites didn't grasp this as a nation, the Lord swore that they would not be able to enter into his finished work.[67]

Much of what we have to receive from God today is directly related to possessing an inheritance. Inheritance implies that we take possession of something we didn't work for. It also implies that someone before our time worked, and accumulated, considerable property, and/or wealth. Through birth, we are entitled to an undeserved and unearned right to what they worked for and accumulated. It's worth whatever effort and expense necessary to get that inheritance.

I firmly believe that more quality time needs to be spent in this area by believers. Whatever we must correct, or improve, in order to receive our inheritance needs to be undertaken. Whatever the cost. Colossians 1:12 states that our heavenly Father has qualified us to be partakers of our inheritance. We are heirs and joint heirs with Christ.[68] If we had received word that a wealthy relative had passed away and left us a considerable inheritance, the expense and effort spent getting to the reading of the will would seem minuscule, compared to the anticipated reward. In the same way, we that are born into the family of God must not spare any expense to possess the inheritance waiting for us. Jesus said, *"Everything that the Father has is mine."* [69] Who can truly conceptualize being an heir to everything God has? If we are to take part in it, we must meditate on this until it becomes real to us. We are called upon to believe and appropriate it for our lives.

What's the revelation here? It is that there is a distinct difference between facts and promises. God has done many things for us that are now facts, not promises. We will certainly waste precious time asking God for things he has already given. Those are prayers that receive little or no response from God. The multitude of things that God has already given, we need to take authority over and possess. Here's an enlightening example:

After months of suffering financially in the ministry, Kenneth Hagin went to God to seek answers. He was told (I paraphrase) that his faith would have to be used not only for healing, but in the area of finances as well. God told him, "Don't pray for me to send you money anymore. The money you need is not in heaven. It's there in the earth. If I printed any up here and sent it down, it would be counterfeit, and I'm not a counterfeiter. Your enemy, Satan, is the one keeping it from you, not me. Command him to release the amount you desire, in the name of Jesus. Then, tell the angels to go and bring it in, because they are your ministering spirits sent to work on your behalf."

What a valuable insight! That revelation totally changed his way of dealing with his need for finances. Hopefully, you also get the point about asking for what is already yours.

CHAPTER SEVENTEEN

BEFORE

"For verily I say unto you, that whosoever shall say unto this mountain, Be thou removed, and be thou cast into the sea; and shall not doubt in his heart, but shall believe those things which he saith shall come to pass; he shall have whatsoever he saith."
                                                                -Mark 11:23

Can you believe that God has designed this life to be one in which you can have whatever you say? The scripture here says just that. The only person we've ever known, that has that kind of power, is God. He spoke in the beginning, and whatever he said, he got. It's a little farfetched to believe just anybody can have that kind of power. After all, God can do anything, because he's God.

This concept is not so unbelievable when you realize you are talking about the sons/daughters of God. We are striving everyday to be like him, growing daily. Our growth will lead to maturity, in which we will be like him. The scriptures declare that when he shall appear, "we shall be like him."[70] His way of doing things is often much different than what we do. I am so impressed that our Father God has left on record how he does what he does. He essentially said that if you want to move even those mountains out there, you will have to say to them certain words, believing that what you say is coming to pass. Speaking words in faith will have to happen **BEFORE** desired changes occur. God has given to us such power in our words, plus we have from him the permission to speak his words.

Faith is not just reading and meditating. It's also regularly exercising by making it a part of your daily speech. But there is a little bit of a twist in how we say what we say. The scriptures declares that with the heart man believes to righteousness, and with the mouth confession is made to salvation. No longer do we say, "Who will go get Jesus and bring him?" But now, the creative Word of God is in our mouths, and in our hearts.

One of the first powerful utterances we make is to confess Jesus as our Lord and Savior. Many mistakenly believe that this is merely a religious moment; in reality, it is much more. This is the beginning of our use of the powerful Law of Confession. That law states that I confess I have obtained the promises of God **BEFORE** I consciously possess them in the natural realm. This way of doing things seems different, because it is different; it's the kingdom way of doing things.

The first time believers use this law is actually when they become believers. As sinners, we say or confess: "Jesus is my Lord." We do that **BEFORE** he acts upon our spirits and recreates them. It's powerful to know our confession moves the ruler of the universe to move on our behalf. He left on record: "Whatever ye bind on earth will be bound in heaven, and whatever ye loose on earth will be loosed in heaven." [71]

Next, to receive the Holy Spirit, we must confess that he has come to live within us **BEFORE** we can expect him to give us the heavenly language of tongues. I used to think just the opposite. I thought you didn't say you received the Holy Spirit, until you spoke fluently in tongues for a while. That's the way I was taught. I feel in some things, God blessed not because of us, but in spite of us.

The same pattern is repeated for healing. You must confess that by his stripes you are healed **BEFORE** the disease and its symptoms leave your body. The symptoms may not leave all at once, but don't be shaken, hold your ground. Your confession of what you believe leads the direction of your life. Whatever you confess—believing—you will possess.

Even in ancient times God was using this law. When he changed the name of Abram to Abraham (father of multitude), he effectively forced everyone around this man of God to exercise faith, by saying what they definitely could not fathom. He was called father of nations decades **BEFORE** the miracle came to pass.

Using this law, our lives will totally change. The Word states that "confession is made to salvation." Salvation implies every aspect of the blessings of God in our lives, not just the assurance of a place in heaven. Right here on earth our confession will have a vital part to play in possessing what is ours.

I heard a true story of a minister who, for three years straight every day, said, "Someone is going to give me a check for one million dollars," as incredible as it may sound. I attended a meeting where this story was confirmed. As a matter of fact, the preacher who relayed the story said that the person who wrote the check asked him for the name of the minister just before he wrote it. I made up my mind to see if this would work for me. I remember speaking that I would receive $15,000. I confessed it over a period of time, months as I recall. Sure enough, one of the members of our group wrote me out a check, from a settlement he had, for that exact amount.

CHAPTER EIGHTEEN

YOU ARE WHAT YOU EAT

"As newborn babes, desire the sincere milk of the word, that ye may grow thereby."

-I Peter 2:2

Having paid the full price for your redemption, Jesus returned authority into your hands. Now God is no longer responsible for what you feed your spirit, your soul, or your body...You are!

In I Thessalonians 5:23, we learned that there are three parts to man: spirit, soul, and body—in that order. Each of these parts must be properly nourished if we are to live a balanced life. The spirit is the highest form, especially since we've been born again. The soul is the mind, the will, and the emotions of man. And the physical body operates by the five senses. With the spirit, we contact God; with the soul, we contact the intellectual realm; and with the body, we contact the physical. In order to grow properly, each part must be fed. The spirit feeds on the Word of God. The soul feeds on all forms of knowledge, and the body feeds on physical food. We will grow in our spirit man if we feed on the Word of God. How do we feed? By reading the Word for ourselves, listening to Bible teachings, reading books, etc.

Many of God's people wonder why they are so weak when it comes to temptation; why they keep losing the battle in their fleshly desires, whether it's the desire for food, or sex, or other things. Why is our physical man overpowering the better judgment of our inner man? It all relates to our eating habits. Romans 12:2 states: *"Be not conformed to this world but be ye transformed by the renewing of your mind."* When we are born again, only our spirits—or hearts—are changed. Our minds have collected a lot of sensual, and natural, junk. They must be renewed. Our bodies must be reprogrammed. We have many misconceptions about many things. The Word of God fed into our spirits will begin to cleanse the misconceptions and bring the light. As we learn about God we learn about ourselves, because we are made like him. Years of deception and wrong thinking, however, will not die easily.

JUNK FOOD

As sweet snacks, chips, and sodas are tasty, but largely "junk food" for the body, so is unregulated television, movies, and pornography to the mind. On the other hand, the Word of God is of benefit in every part. Words evoke pictures. With them we are able to bring concepts of whatever we desire. The Word of God brings pictures on what God is thinking, as well as what he desires for his people.

> *"Beloved I wish above all things that thou mayest prosper and be in health even as thy soul prospereth."*
>
> -III John 1:2

> *"Nothing shall be impossible unto you."*
>
> -Matthew 17:20

> *"With his stripes ye are healed."*
>
> -Isaiah 53:5

The pictures from the mind of God are wonderful for man's mind. As I've stated in a previous chapter, I believe that the mind of man is perfectly designed, mainly, to hold the pictures from the Word. Fearful thoughts can be eliminated by a steady dose of God's word. In tough times, his Word is often the only good news there is. Thinking on his Word brings illumination to the mind, as well as benefits to our bodies. God never meant for us to walk one step at a time in knowledge, but to soar as he soars in wisdom, knowing things that are astounding to the natural mind. Nutritional needs for the informed believer are no longer merely a matter of sustenance for the body. It now involves the three major parts of man: spirit, soul, and body. We must not only select the food we eat, but also what is the feeding priority. If we feed the body most without feeding our spirit, it will become dominant and physical desires will rule. It then becomes very difficult to tell the body "no" when desires come. If we feed the mind secular knowledge without any input from the word of God, our natural wills and intellects will become very strong indeed. As a result, we will begin a strong inclination toward the deception of natural life, and independence from God.

On the other hand, if we feed the spirit with the Word in the same three meals-a-day pattern as the body, wonderful results will occur. Faith is a welcomed result that begins to manifest when we feed on the Word. This is the proper priority. Our whole being will experience life and peace from the entrance of the Word. *"Man shall not live by bread alone, but by every word that proceeds out from the mouth of God man lives."* [72]

CHAPTER NINETEEN

CHANGE YOUR WORDS, CHANGE YOUR WORLD

"But I say unto you, That every idle word that men shall speak, they shall give account thereof in the day of judgment. For by thy words thou shalt be justified, and by thy words thou shall be condemned."
-Matthew 12:36-37

"For verily I say unto you, That whosoever shall say unto this mountain, Be thou removed, and be thou cast into the sea; and shall not doubt in his heart, but shall believe that those things which he saith shall come to pass' he shall have whatsoever he saith."
-Mark 11:23

Early in the Bible, we see the power of words when spoken by God in the creation. God said, "Let there be" and there was. His words created the entire world we now inhabit. The book of Genesis reads like a fantasy to many because fallen man has not known such awesome power in words. As we read on in the scriptures, we begin to see that God's words are more than just utterance from a divine being. They are spiritual law. Like seed, they are planted, and in due season they bring forth a harvest.

Jesus, in the above verses, began to reintroduce man to the power of words, informing his followers that they are not to be used or taken lightly. They are to be active, and not idle or ineffective. He even warned of consequences when they are allowed to be idle. God said, *"My words are gone out of my mouth they shall not return unto me void"* (Isaiah 55:10).

As the children of God, we now must watch our words. Since this is the means designed by God for us to produce good things, then let us use words more carefully.

The enemy loves to get us to speak self-defeating words, words that accept illness, poverty, and defeat as unchangeable conditions. When we do this, we play right into his hands. Since the Word of God is the *"sword of the spirit" (Ephesians 6:17)*, we know this is a very effective weapon for the defeat of Satan. Jesus said to the devil, when he was tempted: *"It is written"* and, *"It is said" (Luke 4:4,12)*. Those words had a noticeably disarming effect on Satan. He was stopped in his tracks, and could no longer continue his attack after his third attempt. Totally spent, the formerly unrelenting master temper, Satan, left the contest and never attempted the strategy against our Lord again.

Since Jesus said we will have whatsoever we say, we can no longer allow any and everything out of our mouths. What comes out of our mouths is what defiles us, Jesus said in Matthew 15:11. Wrong speaking would then be anything said that is not in accordance with the Word of God. In the past, we have said so many things that are contrary to the Word of God. Statements like: "I'm afraid I'll be worried sick over this thing"; "It's killing me!"; "No matter how hard we try, we'll never get ahead"; "Bad things always happen to me"; "Every year around this time I catch the flu. I'll be sick for a few days." Each of these statements, besides being negative in context, are all contrary to the promises of God for our lives. Each ignores the blessings God pronounced over his people, and each denies his great redemptive work. Fear, uncertainty, doubt, and disbelief (What I call the FUDD spirit) should never be allowed to dominate the speech of the child of God. Instead, we should practice speaking what God said about the situation. If we would change our speech, we would find in time that changing our words will change our world.

SECTION FIVE

SECRET SEDUCTION, PUBLIC PAIN

One of my first revelations from the Lord was an incident that happened after I graduated from college. It was not one of my shining moments as a believer, but I learned a serious lesson I will share with you. In 1972, I was hired by the Atomic Energy Commission as a management assistant, about a week before graduation from college. They sent me away for training to Argonne National Laboratory, to expose me to all areas of contract administration. It was a great job; just the kind I wanted that didn't require me to lift anything heavier than a pencil.

At Argonne, all my expenses were paid and I had my own apartment, located within 30 minutes-drive of downtown Chicago. What a set up! I was a single man with no family responsibilities, and very few bills. No one knew me, and no one knew anything about me outside of the Commission. Having been under strict accountability to the church; my parents; and my saved friends, all my life, I was glad to have the freedom this short getaway promised. I enjoyed the country-like setting with an indigenous herd of white deer roaming about, and the solitude of jogging late in the evenings. And although I feared the Lord and was saved to the bone, the opportunity for a secret fling with a female toyed with my thoughts.

I began to focus on it and fantasize about it. It wouldn't be anything meaningful; no commitments: nothing but a couple of days of youthful indulgence. After all, who would know? In my telephone conversations with a more-than-willing sister back in New York, she so brazenly offered to fly out to come and see me. The very thought was exciting to me because she was a few years older than me, and very experienced. I knew that worldly experience would certainly make our meeting so interesting. I could easily pick her up at the airport, and we could spend some time together. She could stay at my place. Of course, we had no intentions of anything happening. This would just be an innocent meeting of two friends. Knowing better, we both lied to ourselves. We flirted on the phone and made plans. My mind raced in anticipation, fighting the nagging fact that I knew this was so wrong. We both knew, but proceeded with planning anyway.

Then late one evening, I received a call from my mother. She sounded sad, and her words were very slow and measured. She said, "Al, I'm calling to let you know that Audrey has come forth and confessed to the pastor that she went to bed with your father. His side of the story is that he went to her place tired. She suggested that he could take a nap before eating the meal she had prepared. Unexpectedly, as he slept, she got into bed with him. All he could say was, 'she tricked me.' The pastor has called a meeting of the church to deal with the matter publicly."

All was silent for a brief moment, then my shock, and disbelief, erupted. "Oh my God," I said, "No, no, no, not Dad?" I felt so keenly my father's utter embarrassment. He was a respected elder in the church, with grown children no less, a straight-laced paragon of virtue to his kids all of our lives. Never would he allow even a hint of wrong doing in his presence. Now he had fallen, not privately, but exposed to the whole church. I felt a sick feeling deep in my gut, of being caught in the very act of doing wrong. Although he was the one who had yielded to temptation, I felt like it was me. Suddenly, God was driving a point home to me. I fell to my knees and repented for the very thoughts I had entertained. Needless to say, my appetite for anything secret or carnal vanished, replaced by remorse. The public humiliation that was soon to be faced by my father, should have been mine, could have been mine, and would have been mine!

It was crystal clear to me now that the price to leaders for a few moments of secret indulgence was way too high. As I recall, there were several episodes of the same issue that year that ended in a public reprimand. But for the grace of God and this serious lesson, I would have been one of them. I had moved far away from church, family, and friends, but I was so thankful God had moved in with me, and protected me from my own devices. While I remained at Argonne, the temptation didn't cease, but for me the consequences were by far too painful a price to pay.

CHAPTER TWENTY

GOD AIN'T DOING NOTHING ABOUT THE DEVIL

> *"Behold I give unto you power to tread on serpents and scorpions, and over all the power of the enemy: and nothing shall by any means hurt you."*
>
> -Luke 10:19

Another critical revelation that totally jarred my thinking, is the fact that God is not going to do anything more about the devil. He's done all he's going to do. God has always had power over the devil. We're the ones who didn't. Solely for our sakes, he defeated Satan and all his demons through his death, burial, and resurrection. And although we certainly spend a lot of time trying to get him to, if we don't use our authority over the enemy, God can't do a thing. The reason is: to do so would violate his Word. He gave the power over the enemy to us. That may come as a shock to you, as it did to me before I read and studied the scriptures a little more.

YOU HAVE TO DO IT

<u>Nowhere in the New Testament scriptures does it state that he or the Father will do anything about the devil.</u> It's written that **YOU** will cast out devils.[73] He gave **YOU** power over all the power of the enemy.[74] **YOU** will resist the devil, and he'll flee from **YOU**.[75] And, **YOU** are to "give no place to the devil."[76] That's because when He rose from the grave and

said, *"All power in heaven and in earth is given unto me,"*[77] he immediately transferred his power to man. Jesus said to his disciples, *"YOU go preach the gospel and I'll be with YOU."* Since he transferred the power to man, **we must now do something about the devil, or nothing will be done.** *"Whatever you bind on earth will be bound in heaven, and whatever you loose on earth will be loosed in heaven."*[78]

Apparently, in a major shift, heaven is taking its cue from what's said and done on earth. Whether we are aware or not, Jesus has delegated his authority on earth to the Church, and he now can work only through the Church, for he is the Head of the Church, "which is his body."[79] The analogy of the body here is critical to our understanding of this shift of power. Physically, the head is attached to the body and rules over it, but is totally subject to its actions to carry out its will. Late at night, you may think of that delicious dessert you left in the refrigerator. You meant to eat some, and you sure would like a taste right now, but your body is tired and wants rest. In all likelihood, you won't be having any tonight. Your head wants it, but your body is not willing. This is the present picture of the Body of Christ. Jesus wants certain things done, but those things aren't happening because his body is unresponsive. Oh, but when the body is in sync with the head, things get done.

THE GREAT REVELATION

From further study of the subject, a great revelation blossomed; the life changing revelation of the authority we have as believers. The first two chapters in the book of Ephesians describe an <u>exceeding great power</u> that has been released in and for man.[80] Man is now described as quickened together with Christ, and raised up, and seated together in heavenly places in Christ.[81] No longer is Jesus alone doing the works of God. Now Jesus has taken the position as head of a large body of believers, working in sync as the Body of Christ. The authority he has, we now have. Since we know Jesus is seated at the right hand of God, it makes this revelation even more astounding. Mankind has actually been elevated into a position of high authority, seated at the right hand of God with Jesus. Again, this is a revelation. We cannot grasp it with our natural minds. We must take time to meditate on it, asking the Lord to illuminate our minds. This is a revelation that has changed everything!

The scriptures bear this out. In Romans 5:17, it is stated that we who receive the gift of righteousness, and the abundance of God's undeserved favor, shall reign in this life through Jesus Christ our Lord. We are to reign in this life. We are in authority.

TAKING AUTHORITY IN CANADA

I read an interesting account of a group of missionaries driving into Canada from the United States. As they approached the checkpoint to cross the border, one of the men in the back seat spoke up and said, "We take authority over the demonic spirit over this region in the name of the Lord Jesus Christ." The man recalling the incident had never heard such a statement, and thought it quite strange, and a little foolish, to do such a thing. As they passed through the checkpoint without incident, he wondered whether it had any effect at all. When they completed their work, he returned back to the United States. Sometime later, he had to make another trip, this time alone. At some point, he realized he would be driving past the same checkpoint. Since he thought the idea was foolish, he made no such declaration as he approached the guard. To his utter astonishment, not only was he stopped; pulled aside; and searched, but he was also delayed. Worse still, it looked like he would actually not be permitted to cross. He was not allowed to pass through, until he took time to make the same declaration over the spirits operating in that region. If such a simple statement of authority was made, with such a decisive effect, what could you do in the area where you live? God ain't doing nothing more about the devil. You are.

CHAPTER TWENTY ONE

BLESSINGS DON'T FALL LIKE CHERRIES

Contrary to popular opinion, I've found that blessings are not like ripe cherries that fall from a tree. If the reverse was true, all we would have to do is get under the tree and the blessings would fall on us. I believe that one of the most disappointing concepts to permeate the church, is the concept that blessings will automatically happen. I can't count the times I've heard the statement, "Whatever blessings God has for you are sure to come to you," or "If God wants you to have something, he will see to it that you get it." After some years of having this preached to me, and waiting for it to happen, I've discovered that neither of these statements are accurate. As a matter of fact, we have Bible history that makes a different statement.

In the Old Testament, God certainly wanted Israel to possess the Promised Land. But the group that was delivered out from the bondage of Pharaoh never inherited the land. Only two of the original million plus souls who left Egypt actually possessed it: Joshua and Caleb.

THE MISCONCEPTION

One would think that godly living should qualify us to receive blessings, and it does. But **qualified** is a few steps short of **receiving**. God promises that if you live right, you will be blessed. *"No good thing will he withhold from them that walk uprightly before him."* [82] Our interpretation of this scripture made us feel that God was in charge of releasing, or withholding, the blessings coming to man. And subsequently, when he determined that we were ready, he was in charge of sending them down. To our thinking, he is the one responsible for delivering the blessings at the right time. But those who believe this are in for a rude awakening. And sadly, they may wake up only after much loss.

No matter how great and wonderful the promises, and how generous they sound, none can ever be received without an act of faith on our part. The Bible is full of promises of health, wealth, success, and deliverance. Expecting them to easily make their way to you is a mistake. In this life, only the curse from Adam's sin is automatic. We are born into sin, and shaped in iniquity.[83]

Blessings will have to be contended for because of:

1) the sacrifice of Jesus to make you an heir, and

2) the intentions of the enemy to thwart your every attempt to collect.

It's not God holding up your blessing. He intends for every individual to receive the inheritance that he sacrificed his son for us to receive and enjoy. But with the same brazen audacity Satan inspires thieves with, to steal the monthly welfare check that belongs to a desperate needy family, this cruel enemy also lies waiting to steal the blessings you so desperately desire. The truth of the matter is, although you have a loving father who has given you complete access to a vast inheritance, you also have an enemy who is determined to block you. His success compounds your misery. You must use the power you have over him to defeat his every move.

POSSESSING IS A VIOLENT ACTION

Possessing the Promised Land sounds like a friendly occupation. But possessing that land was anything but friendly. Israel had to take the land from its present inhabitants who fought to keep it. God had given them his promise, and they used every weapon at their disposal to destroy the inhabitants. It was kill, or be killed in that land. That's the attitude we must not have with people, but against our enemy—the devil. Utter annihilation of every trace of the enemy was their marching order, and must also be ours. The giants in the land of promise frightened the Israelites causing many to turn back. But, God promised them that the land was theirs for the taking. We cannot afford to repeat the same failure.

Many know how to sow offerings and gifts, and we give our moneys and tithes as seeds sown into good ground. In doing so, the Bible promises a bountiful harvest. But how many know what the farmer knows: that harvesting requires much work? Harvest requires effort to bring the increase into the storehouse out from the fields. Proverbs states: *"the **diligent** soul shall be made fat."* [84]

For years, the devil has stolen from us, and we religiously thought it was God who was withholding the blessings until we were ready. We blamed God, as Job thought, *"The Lord giveth and the Lord taketh away."* He, like many during his time, was not aware of the presence of Satan. In the Old Testament, the devil operated with little restraint. His evil deeds were largely undetected. Both the giving and the taking were mistakenly ascribed to God. But the Lord has proclaimed, *"My covenant will I not break, neither alter the thing that is gone out of my mouth."* [85] God therefore cannot break his covenant of blessing with man. He is covenant bound to protect man against all enemies. He simply will not break his covenant with us. Only man can breach such an agreement by operating in fear, doubt, or disobedience.

TAKE BACK WHAT THE DEVIL HAS STOLEN

> *"The kingdom of heaven suffers violence and the violent take it by force."*
>
> -Matthew 11:12

We must, in accordance with this saying, rise to the occasion and take back all that the devil has stolen. We must be aware of who is causing this obstruction, and inform others as well. Our attitudes can no longer be lax regarding our adversary. The Bible advises that we be sober and vigilant. It also states that he will run in terror when firmly resisted.[86]

Jesus told Peter, *"...the gates of hell shall not prevail against you."* [87] We have often interpreted that scripture to mean that nothing the devil brings against us will prevail. On the contrary, "gates" have never been offensive weapons. They are stationary. In ancient times, gates were strong defensive structures. At the approach of an enemy, the people could enter into a walled enclosure and be protected inside the relative safety of gates that could be closed tight. How does this relate to us? Whatever the enemy has, he has stolen, or obtained by illegal means. Jesus named him the thief.[88] Whenever we approach our rightful blessings, he and his army close the gates. He has the mindset that they belong to him. He then does everything he possibly can to keep the stolen possessions from our grasp. However, the Bible declares:

> "When a strong man armed keeps his palace, his goods are in peace. But when a stronger than he shall come upon him he takes from him all his armor wherein he trusted and divides the spoils."
> -Luke 11:21-22

> "Greater is he who is in you than he that is in the world."
> -I John 4:4

Armed with this knowledge, we must rise up in righteous indignation, and take whatever steps are needed to recapture what has always been ours.

Here are a few tips:

1. Stop Listening to the lies of the Devil

The devil is a liar and *the father of lies*.[89] Make no mistake about it. "If he's moving his lips, he's lying," I heard one preacher say. No one can expect to have good thoughts for a bright future listening to anything he has to say. Whenever feelings of depression come, accompanied by thoughts of fear and hopelessness, I know that I've been allowing his words to enter my mind. Beware of the FUDD spirit (The spirit of Fear and Uncertainty, Doubt and Disbelief).

2. Focus on the Word of God

When we stop listening to the enemy, we must fill our thoughts with the Word. The words of God are thoughts from heaven. They are powerful and will give the reader, and the hearer, the view from heaven—God's view. Even in the midst of adversity, God's words will bring peace and a stabilizing force. God's word is God. The Word is all-powerful when we believe it.

3. Make the Decision that You Will Not Quit

"And let us not be weary in well doing for in due season we shall reap if we faint not."

-Galatians 6:9

God cannot lose; if we walk with him, we won't ever lose either. But we must not quit. That's the one condition. Whatever is born of God overcomes the world.[90] There's a song sung by Kenneth Copeland that goes: "I cannot be defeated and I will not quit." Keep those words in mind as you make the decision never to give up.

CHAPTER TWENTY TWO

THE SUCKER PUNCH

"But Jesus said unto her, Let the children first be filled; for it is not meet to take the children's bread, and to cast it to the dogs. And she answered and said unto him, Yes, Lord: yet the dogs under the table eat of the children's crumbs. And he said unto her, "For this saying go thy way; the devil is gone out of thy daughter."

- Mark 7:27

A sucker punch is professional fighting terminology for a blow that a fighter does not see coming. It is an unexpected punch that can knock out the fighter, or severely hurt him, causing him to lose the match. Another descriptive term is being "blindsided," meaning it's coming from a place you can't see. Satan uses this type of punch on believers. It's unexpected and comes out of nowhere, and it's lethal. How one responds to it is the difference between a discouraging defeat, and a brilliant victory.

We need to be careful after a long trial, or a trying day, where we had to use all of our skills, gifts, and knowledge, just to stave off the enemy's determined attack. Somehow, our adversary knows when we're nearing the finish line of victory, or when "due season" has come, and the blessing we have waited for is about to happen. Feeling impending defeat looming ahead, he has one last trick up his sleeve. It's called "offense." He knows that if he can get you to be offended, he can steal the victory right at the finish line.

The woman in the scripture above was desperate for the deliverance of her daughter. She first came after the disciples, then she pursued Jesus. Since the Jews had strict rules against fraternizing with anyone from another nationality (They were considered unclean), she knew she was taking a chance just coming near him. But take the chance she did. With a heartfelt plea, she begged Jesus to deliver her daughter. What Jesus did next is a bit shocking, and somewhat out of character. He blindsided her with the reason her daughter would not be delivered. Shockingly, it was because it's not right to take bread from children to give to dogs. What an insult! He had just called the woman a dog! We don't know where she found the grace, but she seemed unaffected by the barb. She remained focused on the real reason she was there: to get her daughter delivered. Her answer was more graceful and respectful than mine would have probably been. She humbled herself and accepted a low place; she shrugged off the comment, and as a result got exactly what she came for: deliverance from Jesus for her daughter.

If Satan can't get you any other way, he will reach for your emotions. Anger, hurt, embarrassment—anything that will get an emotional rise out of you, he will try to tamper with. Once he has stirred your emotions, he's got you exactly where he wants you. Some people storm off, walking away from the blessing that in a few more moments was about to be theirs.

DAVID'S FINAL TEST

Just before he was to be anointed king, David returned home to a place called Ziklag. It was his refuge from King Saul's army, who had one agenda: to find David and kill him. To his utter dejection, Ziklag had been burned to the ground, and his family had been taken away by the marauding Amelekites. It was the last straw. He had been on the run for his life for years, one step ahead of death, sleeping in open fields, finding food wherever he could, and leading an army of misfits while at the same time striving to live a life that was pleasing to God. To come and find his home destroyed, and his family taken, was more than he and his followers could stand. Totally disheartened, they cried all night. Then, for the icing on the cake, David's men were so overcome with grief, they began to talk of stoning him. This was a serious sucker punch meant to bring David to his demise. He didn't know it, but in a few days he would be king. This would be his last major challenge before he would ascend to the throne. He steadied himself, and encouraged himself in the Lord. He sought the Lord who directed his path, and ultimately delivered him from this catastrophe. In doing so, he survived the blow the enemy sent to knock him out, and countered with a blow of his own. He withstood the offense from his men and focused on his faith in God.

SHE NEVER SAW IT COMING

In Omaha, I met a woman who was stricken with multiple sclerosis. She had contracted it years earlier, and now it was full blown. She was paralyzed from the neck down and had to lay in bed, moving only with the help of her husband or nurse. She had Kenneth Hagin tapes and books by the dozens. Everything he wrote or produced, she had. She had made up in her mind that if he got his healing from paralysis, she would get hers. She would follow his teachings on faith, looking for her healing. Day after day, we stood on the word. I came and read the scriptures to her, and both of our faiths were strengthened through our time together. It was a real challenge to see her in this condition, but she rose to the challenge, and refused to allow any thought to the contrary in her house, or in her presence. We stood together for years believing for her complete healing. One day, I came to visit and she was visibly upset. I closed the door so she could confide in me in private what had caused her sadness. Apparently, a friend had called her and told her that the home her husband was renovating was not just for extra income. It was to move his girlfriend and her child there. I knew Dave. He was no such person. He was devoted to his wife forever. He loved her like no other, and was totally devoted to the death. He spent his life taking care of her. In spite of that, the news had hit home with Carlene, and she was devastated. She believed her friend. From that moment on, everything went spiraling downhill. Although for months we together had fought hard against doubts and all of her physical challenges, she died within a couple of weeks. She did not survive the blow.

HOW CAN ONE SURVIVE SATAN'S SUCKER PUNCH?

1) **Realize that he has it in his arsenal.** Expect it. Especially when you're tired or after a long ordeal—expect an insulting or offensive remark.

2) **Don't make any major decisions when you are angry or offended.** Wait a day or so until you're seeing clearly.

3) **Make up your mind.** It's not about you. You belong to God. They talked about, and insulted, Jesus. Who are you to escape?

4) **Decide no matter what is said, you will not allow offense to throw you off track.** You will walk in love. God's got this!

CHAPTER TWENTY THREE

GOD ISN'T OBLIGATED TO BLESS YOU WHERE HE DIDN'T SEND YOU

God's blessings upon the children of Israel in Deuteronomy, Chapter 28 which includes health; wealth; victory; and rule, were contingent upon them obeying his commandments, and setting foot **<u>in the land which the Lord thy God giveth thee</u>** (verse 8). He repeats this phrase twice to make his point. He was essentially saying to the children of Israel, *"The blessing is waiting on you in the place where I tell you to go"*.

The will of God for our lives includes not only his principles, but a place. When he told Moses and Joshua, "Every place that the sole of your foot shall tread upon that have I given unto you,"[91] he was talking of a specific area—the Promised Land. Blessings are related to specific places that God has planned for us.

Who hasn't heard the story of the consequences of Jonah willfully running away from the place God instructed him to go? Not only was his blessing affected, but he almost lost his life as well. Had he not repented in the belly of the whale,[92] the story's ending might have been much different. Likewise, if we are neglectful of obeying God in the place he has directed us to, unpleasant consequences will happen. This is not so much God punishing us. It's the results of us unwisely straying out from under his area of protection for our lives. When we walk away from his protection, anything can happen, and often does.

When God blessed Elijah with the miracle of the birds bringing his food, he was given a specific place to dwell—by the brook Cherith. And when it was time for a change, he was instructed to go to Zarepath, to the widow with the handful of meal and cruse of oil. The blessing of the Lord came as he arrived in the place where God wanted him. When we are introduced to Abraham in Genesis 12:1, God is instructing him to leave the place he's lived in for some time, and to go to a place he would show him. If he was obedient, God promised to bless him and make his name great. He obeyed, and history is replete with the blessings his descendants are receiving to this very day.

We cannot afford to choose where we're going to live, by what we like, or think, is best. We dare not try to resist God's will when choosing a home. Our blessings lie in the will of God for our lives. It's dangerous to miss God in this matter. His protection from the enemy is located in the place of his will. The anointing we so desperately need flows freely only in the place of his will.

God is not responsible to bless you where he didn't send you. When God sends an individual to a certain area, it becomes obvious to the community that God's hand is upon the work. Before he was so widely known, Bishop T. D. Jakes established a small ministry in Charleston, West Virginia. But when he followed the leading of the Lord and moved to Dallas, Texas; his ministry and appeal increased by thousands.

Mike Murdock wisely stated, "Don't stay where you're tolerated, go where you're celebrated." Jesus could not do many great works in his own hometown. When people did not receive him, he didn't force the issue. He went to areas where he was received.

CHAPTER TWENTY FOUR

BE PREPARED FOR THE COUNTER ATTACK

> *"Then Peter got down out of the boat, walked on the water and came toward Jesus. But when he saw the wind, he was afraid and, beginning to sink, cried out, 'Lord, save me!'"*
>
> -Matthew 14:29-30

Did you know it's possible for you to have a miracle performed in your life from God Almighty, and lose the blessing? I have always believed that if God does something in your life, it's permanent. That's true, but only if you know how to hold on to it. No one wants to think about losing something that God has done for him or her. It's challenging enough to believe God for a mighty miracle, but after experiencing a miracle, to have it taken away is devastating. Our loving Father has expressed through scripture, his great desire to bless his people with what eyes haven't seen, and ears haven't heard. We feel ready for all that God has for us. What some of us are unaware of, and therefore totally vulnerable to, is the enemy's counterattack.

THE THIEF

Nothing that Satan has was ever earned or created by him. Everything was stolen from someone who was blessed by God: from Adam and Eve, who were given the entire earth to rule over, to the present day believer, who has been raised up and seated in heavenly places in Christ.[93] In Jesus' parable of the sower, he stated that when the word is sown, immediately the enemy comes to steal it out of the heart of the hearer.[94] It's time we woke up to this glaring fact. Satan is a thief. How he gets his wealth, property, and influence is by stealing it. If we are aware of this scheme we can be prepared.

In the scripture above, Peter has asked Jesus to let him walk on water. What an opportunity to experience the miraculous power of God! Jesus encourages him to come and walk. Miraculously, Peter walks on water, but to his utter shock, his supernatural experience suddenly and inexplicably comes to an end as he begins to sink. Apparently, he wasn't expecting the wind to be such a force against him. Had he known the wind would be so strong against his advance, he might have been ready. Jesus said that the problem was his faith. Jesus, sometime earlier, had rebuked the contrary winds with the words "Peace, be still."[95] The lesson was he needed to hold his faith steady, even when confronted by the wind.

In the Bible, it is noticeable that immediately after the performance of a great miracle, there's a backlash on its heels. The children of Israel were released by Pharaoh, after the mysterious death of all the first born of Egypt, only to be pursued by the Egyptian army to bring them back. Elijah called down fire from heaven, but ran for his life when Jezebel threatened to take his life. Paul and Silas were arrested, publicly beaten, and thrown in jail directly following the casting out of an evil spirit of divination (fortune teller). And Peter, after walking on water, began to sink. It appears there's more to miracles than we imagined. Because, instead of relaxing at the end of a move of God, we need to remain vigilant. Let's be wise. What better time for an alert enemy to attack God's people, than directly after a miracle when we are in relax mode? Don't be fooled; miracles which begin in faith apparently need faith to be continued.

HEALING ALMOST LOST

All my life, I thought if God healed you, nothing could take that away. I was surprised to hear a testimony from the great faith teacher, Kenneth Hagin, to the contrary. Apparently, after being raised up from a terminal heart condition and paralysis, I never expected to discover that he nearly lost his healing. He said that he started to feel disturbing symptoms from his former illness. He said he found himself, when asked how he felt, responding with just how he felt in his body. And according to his account, each time he responded with the way he felt—which was worse each day—his condition steadily worsened. Then, all of his symptoms, which had disappeared, began to return. Unaware that he was slipping backward, he accepted rides home whenever offered, because people said he looked like he couldn't make it walking. After a few days of this, he found himself in bed more than he was out. It was obvious he was losing his healing.

The solution he found was to completely reverse his words and his actions. Instead of speaking how he felt, he started speaking his healing according to Mark 11:24. When asked if he needed a ride home, even though the temperature was above 100 degrees, he refused and claimed his healing, walking all the way home in the blistering heat. But immediately, he began to regain his divine healing by returning to his stand of faith in God's word.

It's so easy to drift back into walking by our feelings and five senses. Anyone can lose a God given blessing by returning to walking by sight, and talking doubt instead of faith. Miracles require faith, and we should be ready with as much as is needed.

WHAT JESUS DID

Jesus encountered a similar confrontation after his time of fasting in the wilderness,[96] being tempted to use his power to make stones into bread. He resisted the devil by the statement: "It is written. Man shall not live by bread alone, but by every word that proceeds out of the mouth of God." Who would expect the tempter to approach Jesus after a 40 day fast? It's such an unexpected thing. But there he was with a comeback against Jesus. But, unlike many of us, Jesus was prepared for the counterattack when the devil again confronted him, and dismissed him with: "It is also written...." Jesus knew that you have to be ready for the counterattack. After his resistance of the enemy, the scriptures stated that the devil left him, and the angels came and ministered to him.

There have been accounts of individuals receiving divine healing in meetings from terrible illnesses. Many rejoiced and witnessed with their own eyes what God had done. However, sometime later, the illness returned, and in some cases it's much worse. What happened? Some say they were never really healed in the first place. They reason that if God heals you, you're healed for good. The problem is that any move of God requires faith from those who are on the receiving end. That faith has to continue being exercised, or the miracles can be lost. Is it that simple and easy to lose? Only if we are not watchful and allow the enemy to rob us. Our enemy is a known thief. He steals, kills, and destroys. Everything he has is stolen from someone.

Don't be naïve; hard fought ground (whether healing or other miracles) can be lost unless we remain on guard and keep our faith going. Even after God has answered your prayer, be on guard against the counterattack of the enemy. If we remain vigilant, and understand the strategy of our enemy, we will not lose any ground.

Take note of what Jesus says in Matthew 12:43-45 about the mindset of our enemy:

> *"When an evil spirit comes out of a man, it goes through arid places seeking rest and does not find it. Then it says, "I will return to the house I left." When it arrives, it finds the house unoccupied, swept clean and put in order. Then it goes and takes with it seven other spirits more wicked than itself, and they go in and live there. And the final condition of that man is worse than the first. That is how it will be with this wicked generation."*

Being aware of the devices and strategies of our enemy, and taking time to learn about our enemy's patterns, are common sense actions that will certainly keep us from losing the blessings that are ours.

SECTION SIX

WHEN MY FAITH HELD

At times, I have prayed for people with all the faith I could muster, believing they would recover, but they died. The morning after such a night, of desperately holding on to the horns of the altar, left me momentarily empty. I could not escape the disappointment. We needed so badly, but did not get, a miracle. Now we had to deal with the aftermath. As the man of God, I often had to put the best face on the outcome. That's why I longed for the miracles Jesus performed. What it would have meant to me to plan a celebratory feast, instead of another tearful funeral. Worse still, was the fact that now the doubters could smirk and say, "We told you not to get your hopes up. Minister So and So prayed too, and died the same way."

Detecting a hint of weakness in my resolve, doubts as big as city buses often came barreling into my mind, ramming my beliefs, trying hard to dislodge the precious faith I had nurtured and built up through the years. As a result, I felt the full measure of a depressing tidal wave doing its best to overwhelm me with hopelessness. These doubt bullies never came one at a time. They've always ganged up on me at the same time I wondered how to pay $1200 in bills, with $500 in my account; or how to deal with alarming symptoms of sharp pains on the left side of my body, signaling the beginning of a heart attack; or dealing with the bewildered phone call in the night reporting, "The cancer has returned and it's stage four"; or the one every parent of a young adult male child (especially African American) dreads: the news that my son had been arrested on charges of possession of drugs. The worst thing in those instances would be to let my mind entertain hopelessness; it dogged my tracks at every turn. And I dared not let any word of doubt, or self-pity, out of my mouth. Instantly, a swiftly formed downward spiral was evident. Instead, in the midst of my troubles, I could look out and see others receiving unexpected checks, buying new homes, and claiming new testimonies. So, I decided to put on a smile and rejoice with them. It felt like I was hitchhiking a ride on their blessings while I waited and believed for mine. It was tough, but I rejoiced when their money came, rode in their new cars, and shouted as their blessings manifested. What happened as a result, slowly, money came and symptoms disappeared, and after months of deliberations, the case was thrown out of court and my son was exonerated with a clean record.

CHAPTER TWENTY FIVE

WHY AREN'T YOU RECEIVING

God has given us great and precious promises to provide access to experience his divine nature.[97] Whoever will receive his promises as real and act on them, will have the manifestation of them in their lives. The Christian life is filled with the challenge of bringing these promises to pass. But God no longer has to do anything to produce something special for us. He has sent everything we need. There's no longer a problem with the sending (if there ever was). Now the problem is how we receive his Word. Have you ever wondered, "Why am I not receiving?"? The degree to which we prepare a special place for his Word in our lives determines the degree of success we will experience here.

Jesus spoke on one occasion of the parable of the sower.[98] In it he describes what a farmer in those days encountered when planting seed. Since they were mostly farmers, everyone could relate to what he was saying on a natural level. However, a much more important lesson was being taught on a deeper spiritual level, which he revealed when he explained the story. He said that the seed is the Word of God. As the farmer's entire quality of life is dependent upon the successful maturation of the seed, so are our lives upon the success of the Word. And what the farmer experiences, preparing the ground for optimum results, is similar to what we all experience when preparing the proper conditions for the Word to come to pass in our lives.

THE REPUTATION OF THE WORD

The reputation of the Word of God is that it will always produce when received with due reverence. The Word is not just an expression. It is actually God in the earth. It dominates all physical circumstances, and changes them, in accordance with the will of God and the faith of the believer. Isaiah said that it's as the rain that waters the earth and makes it bring forth and bud, that he may give seed to the sower, and bread to the eater. He further stated that it shall not return to him void, or without accomplishing its stated mission or purpose.[99] The Word will do its job every time.

The parable ends with varying degrees of success. The Word produced 30, 60 and 100 fold. Obviously the 100 fold was the best result. But the fault was not in the seed. Its reputation earned over the centuries of mankind's history is intact. Even when circumstances were contrary to it, the Word of God always prevailed. With such a powerful substance, how can anyone neglect to capitalize on its proven track record?

PROVIDE PROPER CONDITIONS FOR THE WORD

There is nothing more important in our lives than the effort we expend making sure we provide proper conditions for the Word of God to bring manifestation. In so many cases of terminal illness, abject poverty, and overwhelming adversities, there is just no other hope. It's sad, but many feel that there are other priorities that outrank adequately preparing for proper manifestation of the Word. Others have already surrendered the portion of the Word they heard, not even bothering to dig to find understanding. They don't understand that faith comes by it, which is the substance for all miracles. So the enemy swoops down like a bird after seed, and takes the "miracle seed" out of their hearts. He well understands the lasting defeat he experiences each time the Word matures and manifests. It is both alive and powerful.[100] The various mediocre experiences that occur when people receive the Word, demonstrate a blindness to its miraculous power and life changing ability.

Nevertheless, Jesus repeated the ancient edict that *"Man shall not live by bread alone but by every word that proceeds out of the mouth of God"*.[101]

God has blessed man *"with every spiritual blessing in the heavenly realm"* [102] when he gave us the use of his word. Jesus said prophetically, *"If ye abide in me, and my words abide in you, ye shall ask what you will, and it shall be done unto you."* [103] Our responsibility is clear here: to have his words abiding in us. The Word is God. Since we have been given the use of the creative force that made the world, and that dominates the enemy, we must protect its place in our hearts.

The problem is no longer on the sending end. The problem is the receiving of the Word. It is no longer how we react to our circumstances, but how we treat the Word in the midst of the circumstances.

> *"Be careful (anxious, worried) for nothing but in everything through prayer and supplication with thanksgiving let your requests be made known unto God. And the peace of God which passes all understanding shall keep your heart and mind through Jesus Christ our Lord."*
>
> -Philippians 4:6

CHAPTER TWENTY SIX

BEWARE OF THE FAITH LOOK ALIKE

Agreeing with the Word of God mentally is a good thing, but it's not faith. It more accurately describes mental assent. Faith comes from the heart, not the mind. Romans 10:10 states: *"with the heart man believeth..."* Jesus spoke about believing in the heart. He said, *"Whosoever shall say unto the mountain be thou removed and be thou cast into the sea and shall not doubt in his heart, but shall believe those things he saith shall come to pass he shall have whatsoever he saith."* [104]

Mental assent is what so many people have been mistaking as faith. They all mentally agree that God's Word is true. Because of that, they consider themselves believers. The problem is very little happens with just mental agreement. Faith comes from the heart: *"For with the heart man believes."* [105] It comes from the inner man, and is beyond natural intellect and natural feelings.

John Wesley is reported to have said that the devil has given the Church a substitute for faith that looks, and sounds, so much like faith, many people can't tell the difference. He called it "mental assent." Mental assent says I know God's Word promises me healing. I know God's Word is true. I don't understand why I can't receive my healing, or the answers to my prayers. Faith in God's Word says, "I believe God's Word is true. His Word says I'm healed. Therefore I believe I receive my healing now."

> *"For as the body without the spirit is dead, so faith without works is dead also."*
>
> -James 2:26

Faith is inactive and merely a mental exercise unless there is corresponding action. Action is what separates real faith and mental assent. The woman with the issue of blood said within herself, *"if I may but touch his clothes, I shall be whole."* She pressed her way to do what she had said. Faith was in that action. Jesus told her after her healing, "Thy faith made thee whole."[106] Her faith, which was demonstrated by a corresponding action, made her whole. Action is key to results in faith. David said to Goliath, *"this day I will take your head off of your shoulders and feed your body to the beasts of the field and the birds of the air."* [107] Then he gathered stones from the brook and ran toward the giant. We are all familiar with the miracle of the giant being defeated by a shepherd boy with a sling. God requires an act of faith in every battle and in every contest. The army of Saul had any number of men who could have done what David did. But they didn't. David did not have a monopoly on using a sling. He knew, however, that if he would provide action with his declaration, God would back him up.

Without corresponding action, faith is dead and useless, merely mental assent. We can all do something to give action to our faith. God waits for it. Apparently, he needs it to form the miracle. He said, "My strength is made perfect in weakness."[108] Isn't it humbling to have a God who requires our human action before he can intervene? God takes our "natural" act and adds his "super, to make our outcomes supernatural. We must give God something to work with. It's almost as if when we come to God with a request, he looks at us with anticipation saying, "OK, where is it? Where's your faith action?"

CHAPTER TWENTY SEVEN

FEAR CONTAMINATES FAITH

"For God has not given us the spirit of fear, but of power and of love and of a sound mind."

- II Timothy 1:7

"Fear tolerated is faith contaminated."

-Kenneth Copeland

It is a relatively little known fact that fear contaminates faith. But this little known revelation is the likely answer to the question of why so many hastily constructed last minute cries or prayers were ineffective. In the "Superman" comic strip, it only took one bit of kryptonite to sap the strength of Superman. Whenever he lost his strength, the reader knew that a kryptonite stone was somewhere in the area. Likewise, fear contaminates faith, making it useless. That's why in some cases, it seemed as though it took a whole truckload of it to get results. According to Jesus, faith only the size of a mustard seed is potent enough to move mountains.[109] Unfortunately, sometimes we're not asking in faith, but in fear.

When it comes to healing, people often put up an appearance of faith when actually, they're just scared: frightened of hospitals and doctors, needles and operations. Supposedly standing on faith, they resolutely declare never to go to the doctor. But any such declaration disguised as faith will not yield the desired results. At some point fear must be faced. Doctors can be very helpful in pinpointing, diagnosing, and treating an illness. We need to know exactly what's wrong so we can stand in faith for our healing. Avoiding them because of fear is a serious mistake. On the other hand, we must stand in faith believing for our healing, no matter what the diagnosis. We believe the report of the Lord that says, "With his stripes we are healed."[110]

Growing up in a family of seven children, with a father who worked as a presser in a dry cleaners, money was always scarce. Going to the doctor or dentist was pretty much a luxury we could not afford. Only bleeding emergencies, or childbirth, would qualify for a visit. I had asthma growing up. Since we could not afford treatment, I would just endure the shortness of breath and wheezing until it subsided, which usually took about two or three days. During my ordeal, I wanted so badly to be healed because I had to pull for every breath. Days afterward, my chest would be tired, and sore, from pulling for air all night long. The experience certainly shaped my life. I hate sickness and what it does to people. I have dedicated my life to learn about healing. However, I have never been afraid of doctors, nor hospitals. I have learned the great value they bring, but I'm not limited to their limitations. Regular check-ups are a wise practice, and there are some medications that help nicely with the discomfort of pain. Having said that, I am always looking for the supernatural hand of God to prevail when medical science has exhausted its resources.

LOVE FLUSHES OUT FEAR

The Lord knows our hearts. Man looks on the outward appearance, God looks at the heart.[111] It is to our advantage to begin to face the fear, and be honest with ourselves regarding it. Pray: "Lord I need your help with this one. I sense that I have fear in this area. I know that you did not give us the spirit of fear. I therefore resist fear in the name of Jesus Christ. I know that I am healed by the stripes of Jesus. I am willing to go through this, knowing that you are with me." Then take time to meditate on the scriptures on the love of God for us: "Perfect love casts out fear."[112] Getting rid of fear is more than just rebuking the devil. It's strengthening our relationship with God—who is love; that will eventually flush out fear. Once we realize the extent of his love, and the lengths he has gone through and will go through to protect us from danger, fear will lose its grip. Confidence will replace fear.

Whenever the Lord appeared to an individual in the Bible, one of the first things he would say is "fear not." Fear paralyzes the child of God, and blocks God from communicating with him. Fear is faith heading speedily in the wrong direction. It is faith in our destruction, and in the ability of the enemy over us. Fear is faith in the strength, knowledge, and strategy of the devil. Fear is as valuable to Satan as faith is to God. It is the reverse of faith. By it the enemy does his destructive work on mankind, constantly scheming to inject his poison everywhere there's an opening. As faith attracts miracles, fear attracts destruction. Without it, the devil is exposed as an imposter. With it, he continues his deception, influencing the lives of people under his oppressive rule.

Throughout the history of man, fear has been present, except at the very beginning. There was no fear then, and no need for it. Adam's communion with God was uninterrupted. But upon the separation of God from Adam, death came, and fear on its heels. Separation from God, even for a moment, summons fear because man is unprotected and on his own. Cursed with an uncertain future with an unseen enemy, and living in an uncontrolled environment, man immediately became the prey of Satan.

Jesus came and reconciled us to God and revived our dead spirits. He then returned us to our authority over the devil and his cohorts. He has not given us the spirit of fear, but of power. With it we can now live fear free, which is our original state. When we live free from fear, we're moving in our God designed heritage.

We must face our fears and defeat them, like David faced Goliath. Praying to avoid confrontation with what we fear, often is just a delay in an inevitable appointment. What we fear will continue to hound us. Once faced and defeated, fear has no foundation for torment. Fear is a spirit that is not to be tolerated. In this day, much has been done in the name of terror. But the Lord said in Isaiah 54:14, *"...you shall be far from oppression, for you shall not fear and from terror for it shall not come near you."*

CALAMITY STRIKES

As we all watched helplessly, Brittney, my three year old daughter, slipped from her mother's grasp and fell down two 10 foot sections of steep, old, hardened wooden stairs, tumbling uncontrollably to the cold concrete landing below. It was heartbreaking to watch our precious little baby girl receiving those cruel blows from each step, then the next, then the next. My wife, Debby, had tried frantically to grab her hand just before she slipped, but was a split second too late.

As suddenly as it began, it ended with Brittney lying motionless at the bottom of the stairs. Certain of broken bones or worse, Debby immediately wilted to the floor shrieking in anguish. Her cry was not only for the injured baby, but for the fact that she totally blamed herself for her inability to prevent it. For she had only been distracted for a moment, and that was all the time needed for this calamity to pay us a visit.

I had made up my mind long before this that I would never be so close to my children, that I could not function if something happened. My children have meant so much to me. It stood to reason that the enemy would one day attack my faith by trying to hurt one of them. I had steeled myself to this possibility, and prepared my faith to stand should it happen. I began praying and standing on his promises, as I scooped her limp body from the concrete and rushed her to the Emergency. Strangely, I had no fear, but a steady peace governed all my actions.

Remarkably, after a thorough medical examination, Brittney showed no trace of the terrible tumble she had just taken. There were no broken bones, no ugly scars, nothing but a slight redness on her forearm. I truly believe the outcome would have been much more tragic had I allowed fear to enter the situation.

CHAPTER TWENTY EIGHT

THE MASTER KEY: CONTROLLING YOUR THOUGHTS

"For the weapons of our warfare are not carnal, but mighty through God to the pulling down of strong holds; Casting down imaginations, and every high thing that exalteth itself against the knowledge of God, and bringing into captivity every thought to the obedience of Christ;..."

- I Corinthians 10:4-5

It was awesome for me to learn that one of the most effective weapons we have as believers, is the one that gives us the power to regulate the very thoughts that come through our minds. Early in my saved life, I believed that my mind could roam wherever it wanted. Sinful thoughts would come to me, and as long as I didn't act on it, I felt I was alright. "After all," I rationalized, "who can control his/her mind?" It is commonly believed that very little can be done about our thought lives. However, according to the Word of God, the power to "cast down imaginations" is ours. When we exercise this weapon, we also are exercising God's power to pull down strongholds. A stronghold is defined as a mindset impregnated with hopelessness, which causes the believer to accept as unchangeable, that which he knows is contrary to the will of God. I found it helpful to memorize this definition.

It is quite disturbing in our walk with God when we notice that after a glorious salvation, old thoughts and habits return. Paul said in Romans

12:1-2: *"I beseech you therefore, brethren by the mercies of God, that ye present your bodies a living sacrifice, holy and acceptable unto God which is your reasonable service and be not conformed to this world but be ye transformed by the renewing of your mind."* As we renew our minds with the Word of God, our entire lives will be transformed. There's nothing comparable to the Word of the Lord that can transform lives. But the Word must be read, heard, and meditated in order for its benefits to take hold.[113]

THOUGHTS ARE LIKE BIRDS

I once heard a speaker describe thoughts as being similar to birds in flight. He said, "You can't keep them from flying around your head, but you can surely stop them from making a nest in your hair." Ungodly and fleshly thoughts are often uninvited and unwelcomed visitors that exercise a strong influence over our lives. Proverbs 23:7 states: *"As a man thinketh in his heart so is he."* The thoughts we allow will shape our lives. Scores of thoughts of all shapes, sizes, subjects, and varieties cross our minds every day. Some of them can be quite shocking, especially when they resurface in an area we thought we had under control. Old lusts and habits, former temptations and alluring attractions, even vivid memories of past failures, embarrassments and/or humiliations too often walk through our minds as if we had summoned them. If left to roam freely, ungodly thoughts cause serious damage. Often serving as tools of the enemy, carnal thoughts can keep us in bondage and tormenting fear.

Can anything be done to stop them from just walking into our consciousness? Yes. We can be the master over our thoughts. Every believer can stand guard over the thoughts that enter his consciousness, and immediately reject those that are from the enemy. Those thoughts that leave us reeling with fear, doubt, and uncertainty should be rejected outright. Thank God we can cast down the unwanted imagination, and bring every thought into obedience of Christ. When unwanted thoughts come, we must say, "I resist you in the name of Jesus. I cast you down out of my mind in Jesus' name." Then we stand our ground. Since it was sent from the devil it must go.[114] What a relief and blessing this is to the entire Body of Christ.

Because he has operated in the area of our flesh (five senses) and our souls (mind, will, and emotions) for so long, Satan has enjoyed unlimited access to our thoughts. We must begin to deny him that access. A good place to start would be to curtail the time we spend receiving unrestricted thoughts that come from too much TV. No thought should be able to remain in your mind without your approval. Although he can send thoughts to your mind, the enemy does not know what you are thinking at all times. Only when you open your mouth and let him know, is he made aware of what you really feel. So we ought to measure our words and treat evil thoughts as intruders.

Our thoughts shape who we are and how we react to everything. In the Old Testament, because the Israelites thought of themselves as grasshoppers in the sight of their enemies, they were paralyzed with fear and could not possess the land promised to them by God. Our minds hold pictures and images, and our bodies respond to those pictures and images. Whatever the image, whether good or evil, if it remains in our minds, our bodies will react. Our bodies cannot help but respond to the thoughts we hold. Even when we dream our bodies react. Sometimes we're so glad to wake up and realize what we experienced was only a dream. Other times we have awakened in a cold sweat, because our bodies don't differentiate between what is real and what is only a dream.

DESIGNED SOLEY FOR THE WORD

Our minds are perfectly designed and suited for the Word of God. Images and pictures flowing from the scriptures come from heaven, from the mind of God. When received by our minds, the Word is like seeds planted in the soil. It starts the process of manifestation. The Word planted in our minds, through studying and meditation, produces the substance of faith, which drives out fear. It even ushers in healing, and brings peace to our lives.

There is an old English expression found in the King James Bible that says, *"take no thought for tomorrow."*[15] It means don't worry about tomorrow, but the way it's stated makes a good point. Take no thought! Thoughts will surely come, but we certainly don't have to take them in.

It's wonderful to know that in Christ we actually have a choice when it comes to thinking. So many problems can be stopped by rejecting the thought when it appears. Stop it early, and we won't have to deal with it later. "*Sin has no dominion over us.*" [116] The Bible even has a list of things to think on:

> "*...whatsoever things are true, whatsoever things are honest, whatsoever things are just, whatsoever things are pure, whatsoever things are lovely...think on these things.*" [117]

It is interesting to note that when an evil spirit is cast out of an individual, he walks through dry places.[118] His desire and intentions are to return home. Our thoughts either provide a place for him to return, or evict him permanently. Carnal thoughts and mindsets give the enemy material with which to rebuild his shelter. They are not subject to the laws of God, and therefore make a suitable dwelling for the enemy of God. Any darkness in our thinking gives the enemy this opportunity.

We aren't always innocent bystanders when it comes to thoughts. Much too often, our minds are realms of retreat into fantasies that we enjoy. Receiving so much sensory enticement from the world in which we live, such as: TV; internet; magazines; videos; and movies, the unguarded mind doesn't stand a chance. It is quite easy to engage in a world of vanity by just sitting in front of a TV, most of which is not real. The principle characters are often actors on a movie set. We have often intentionally reserved a place where we can run wild, without anyone else knowing what we are indulging. But the scriptures plainly state that "*the carnal mind is enmity against God for it is not subject to the laws of God neither indeed can be*" (Rom. 8:7). Therefore, guard your thought life. Whatever you think about will affect your life. Let the Word of God live in your mind.

CHAPTER TWENTY NINE

PERMISSION GRANTED

"But I speak this by permission, and not of commandment."
-I Corinthians 7:6

"For the kingdom of heaven is as a man traveling into a far country, who called his own servants, and delivered unto them his goods....."
–Matthew 25:14

Far too many honest believers are stuck in mediocre positions and predicaments, living lives that are routine, uneventful, and in a word "boring." Not because of the lack of a dream of doing great things for God, or of the accompanying desire that fuels the flame. But for some unexplained reason, although they feel great compulsion to dream, they feel no authority to act. As a result, their dreams lie dormant and inactive, disengaged from the vital action that will cause it to explode on the scene. And what tragedy it is when at the end of their lives, those dreams dissipate like vapor into a vast wasteland of unfulfilled wishes.

In our dreams lie all the potential required for our life assignment. In them is the life designed by our maker, full of challenges and triumphs. Not one defeat is in the plan, not one. I believe dreams are God's divine deposit into our earthly account, to be withdrawn with confidence and commitment, then developed throughout our lives. The alternative is an insufferably mundane existence, which ends with heaven as the final rescue from the prison of the ordinary.

The tragedy in this is that believers by virtue of their faith in God have great opportunities well within their grasp. The reason for failing to benefit from them is so simple, it's almost embarrassing. Many believers have no idea they simply need something called permission.

We have been given full <u>permission</u> by God to be all that he has made us capable of being. The problem seems to be our hesitance to walk in that wonderful <u>permission</u>. The scripture states in St. John 1:12 *"...as many as received him, to them gave he the power to become the sons of God."* This subject is intentionally last, not because of its unimportance, just the opposite. It is so critical to the success of every believer that having conquered all other hindrances, this one will keep the believer stymied in inactivity and ultimate failure, unless understood and mastered. <u>Permission</u> for our purposes can be defined as an act, ritual, or event that grants authority for a change in our behavior. Until permission is given, old behaviors remain, nothing new can occur. Baptism, ordination, graduation, weddings: are all forms of public permission to change behavior. Some are formalized rituals that have their origin in ancient practices. Others are popularly recognized events that hold an important meaning for all involved. But to the individual serving God, it is of the utmost importance to know that God has given permission to accomplish feats we have never dreamed of actually doing. The reason we're not experiencing a higher standard of accomplishments is that relatively few people are aware that permission has already been given. Permission comes with the dream God gave you.

This little recognized, but highly effective, component of success is without equal in its ability to either propel an individual into their God given assignment, or in its absence, stop them in their tracks. Without it, believers are like fully loaded ships that never set sail. "Lack of permission is a primary cause of 'unexplainable failure.' We are as blind to it, as a fish is to water; as a sinner is to sin."[*]

---

[*] *The Seven Spiritual Secrets of Success*, Richard Gaylord Briley, Thomas Nelson Publishers.

MISSED OPPORTUNITY

The scripture in Matthew 25 is a familiar parable about the expectations of the master toward his servants in his absence. In the story, the master delivers his money to his servants and departs for a season. That's something every slave dreams of: having the use of the master's money with the master out of town. Two of the servants understood perfectly what was expected. They took the liberty of investing the master's money and receiving one hundred percent profit for their actions. The third servant buried the money given him, and did nothing. Upon the master's return, the third servant presented the very coin(s) given to him that he had hidden. His actions displeased the master and he was severely reprimanded. The fact that the master's money had been entrusted into the hands of the servants, showed the confidence the master willingly placed in them. The implication was that in the master's absence, the servant failed to capitalize on the permission he had been afforded. Instead of being rewarded as handsomely as the others, he was punished. That servant failed to take full advantage of permission.

From the time we enter this world, we must submit to someone's authority. Permission is required at every turn when we are children. We learn to check for permission for everything we need and everything we want to do. After years of having this so completely ingrained into our minds, is it any wonder that as adults we still have an inward need for it? As we grow older, our fear of the unknown, and our upbringing, underscore its continued influence over us. But in later life, the sooner we obtain permission for our actions, the sooner we discover happiness and success.

Jesse Duplantis, a well-known evangelist, spoke of his frustration when asking God for direction in a certain matter. He was frustrated at the fact that when he asked God for the direction, he heard nothing. As he pressed God on the issue, he was surprised at the answer he received. The Lord told him, "I trust you. The reason you haven't heard any response is because I will back you in whatever you decide." He had been unaware that God trusted him to make good decisions. God is strong enough to make up any deficiencies we might have. The will of God for our lives has been described, not as a confining passage, but as vast as the ocean. We are to sail freely until we run into land. Another analogy is that God's will is a long succession of green traffic lights. We should keep driving until we come to a red light. The book of Acts is filled with the journeys of Paul evangelizing the then civilized world without restriction, until he started for Asia and was forbidden by the Holy Ghost.[119] Paul took full advantage of the permission to go into all the world and preach the gospel. God provided the brakes when it was time to change course.

FROM OBEDIENCE TO FAVOR

God spends significant amounts of time teaching his people obedience, but once that lesson has been learned, promotion comes. Israel in the Old Testament was first taught the laws of God. Obedience was key. But after a period, God totally discontinued his focus on the law. The dispensation of the law progressed to a time of grace or undeserved favor. Under grace, we are not only expected to be familiar with the law, but also to begin to advance to the favor of God and exercise our liberty. Some believers are yet hung up with the obedience aspect of God. They continue to spend time learning and relearning principles of obedience, not realizing that as they do so, the wonderful next step of permission is being totally ignored. As religious duty and commitment, they look for another command or a new instruction to follow, wasting precious time. God, on the other hand, is expecting that by now they have been in training long enough to step out and do good works, without being given a command.

The resurrection of Jesus is the best example of this phenomenon. Before Jesus rose from the grave, life had no promise beyond the present. As a result, men strove desperately to leave an heir to continue their name in the earth. With no hope beyond the grave, death was final. But when Jesus rose from the grave, displaying his power over death, that one event gave men permission to attempt feats never before even considered. They could now move with courage, and boldness, even in the face of imminent death, with little regard for their ancient nemesis. Christ had defeated death and now the possibilities were endless. Men and women could now experience freedom from all enemies and, truly as Jesus has stated, nothing would be impossible.

Permission appears to be a basic human need without which there is no inward authority to act on what we believe to be true. Although mentioned throughout the Bible, this critical element to success has for the most part remained invisible. Faith is the substance of things hoped for. Permission lies somewhere between faith and hope. Permission is the trigger that turns hope into faith. Without it believers are like the driver who sits in the car revving up the engine, but unable or unwilling to take the necessary action to engage the wheels to get the automobile in motion.

We now have a little more insight as to why the wicked prosper. They race ahead taking immediate advantage of the same opportunities offered to believers who are immobilized by the need to check back for permission. Living more recklessly than most of us, the unrighteous give little thought to the consequences of their actions. Because of significantly less inhibitions, they require less permission before stepping out. It is a sad fact that while the wicked are already enjoying the fruits of getting in on a good thing, the righteous are busy getting approval. There is a natural advantage for the one who can enter a competition without having to check back for permission. It was never the Lord's intention for his children to lag behind in any area of life. Permission was given long ago, but success will continue to elude us if we don't believe it.

SECTION SEVEN

I'M GIVING YOU BACK TWENTY YEARS

I would not have chosen the path I have walked. But having walked through it now, I wouldn't take anything in place of it. God pays well for your suffering in unexpected ways. Like many others, I have experienced some difficult challenges and some disappointments, but in fairness to God, I must say that suffering hardship as a servant of the Lord is still so much better than the best the world has to offer. When I suffered for any length of time, God always found a way to make it worth my while.

I remember, on one occasion, we were living in depressing, overcrowded conditions with very little prospects of any immediate relief. I was standing in front of the bathroom mirror, when He spoke to me. He said "I'm giving you twenty years back." I wouldn't have paid much attention to it, and would have passed it off as just my own wandering mind if he hadn't repeated it clearly three times. "I'm giving you twenty years back," he said. I immediately went and shared it with my wife. She gave me a look that said, "Here's this crazy man talking faith again." I must admit, it was difficult hearing any promise with daily difficulties screaming so loudly. But over the succeeding years, whenever I have felt like God left me out of the blessing, I could look in the mirror and see that, although my miracles had yet to manifest, he was keeping his word to me. It is noticeable that God has held back the aging process for me. The older I get, the more this unexpected blessing means to me. He has kept his word. I have also noticed a remarkable physical rejuvenation. God has restored the years the locust has eaten. I call it my personal "in the meantime blessing."

CHAPTER THIRTY

FORGIVENESS ENSURES THE FLOW OF POWER

"And when ye stand praying, forgive, if ye have ought against any: that your Father also which is in heaven may forgive you your trespasses. But if ye do not forgive, neither will your Father which is in heaven forgive your trespasses."

-Mark 11:25-26

Directly following Jesus' teachings in this scripture on moving mountains by speaking words, and praying believing that you receive, Jesus makes the point for forgiveness. Why he attaches it to these teachings is a little disturbing. Everyone wants to have the power to remove obstacles through a spoken word. Everyone also wants prayers to be answered, and to receive the things prayed for. But Jesus brings up the subject of forgiveness as condition required for his teachings to work. The implication here is, while we are eager to use our faith to move mountains and to get prayers answered, don't forget to forgive. Such a condition affects the way God, who is the source of miracles, responds to us.

Jesus taught his disciples to pray, *"And forgive us our debts as we forgive our debtors."* He continues in the same passage[120] to make the point, at the end of the Lord's prayer, to say, *"For if ye forgive men their trespasses, your heavenly Father will also forgive you: But if ye forgive not men their trespasses, neither will your Father forgive your trespasses."* This gives insight into the way God works, as well as the reason some prayers don't. Signifying that God will respond to us in matters of forgiveness the way we respond to those who have committed sins against us. In other words, when we erect the wall of un-forgiveness against someone, we are not just closing them out. By the same act, we are doing great harm to ourselves by shutting out God, who is our source and our supply. It has been rightly stated that holding un-forgiveness and malice in your heart against someone, is **like drinking poison hoping the other person will die**.

Forgiveness appears to be such an important spiritual principle that when applied, releases the blessings of God toward man. Ephesians 4:32 states: *"And be ye kind one to another, tenderhearted, forgiving one another, even as God for Christ's sake hath forgiven you."* The entire work of redemption rests on the decision of God to forgive us of the multitude of sins we have committed. His great love was the foundation for his forgiveness. He did this so effectively that the sins are no longer in his memory. Isaiah 43:25 states: *"I, even I, am he that blotteth out thy transgressions for mine own sake, and will not remember thy sins."* Forgiveness gives man a clean slate upon which to start his new life in Christ Jesus. How often have we made mistakes, and wished that we could start over with a clean slate? God forgives our sins and allows us a fresh start: "Old things are passed away, behold all things are become new."[121] God apparently wants us to do the same for others. He sets the standard high by saying to his disciples to forgive "seventy times seven."[122]

Jesus understood that forgiveness causes healing. He said, "Whether is easier, to say, Thy sins be forgiven thee; or to say, Rise up and walk?"[123] We see from this statement that, to Jesus, forgiveness of sins was synonymous with, or the same thing as, divine healing. Apparently, whenever sin is forgiven, and taken out of the way, physical healing is the result.

My mother told me a story of a preacher who was called to the bedside of a woman dying of cancer. In the course of ministering healing to her, the Lord spoke to him and said, "Tell her if she will forgive her husband, I will heal her." He immediately told the woman what God said. He thought surely she will follow this simple instruction and be healed. But he was shocked to hear her vehemently refuse saying, "No. I will never forgive him for what he did. Never." Needless to say, she died shortly thereafter, but would have lived if she had only found it in her heart to forgive.

CHAPTER THIRTY ONE

THE POWER OF NOW

Years ago in Omaha, Nebraska, I was doing some teaching on divine healing. Shortly after the teaching, to my surprise, I became quite ill with an unknown condition that caused my throat to swell to the point that I could not swallow without intense pain. The pain was so severe that it kept me awake for days. Each attempt to swallow, even the smallest amount of liquid, was torture. I fought the sickness with the scriptures I had taught, but nothing seemed to bring relief.

I am seldom "under the weather" unless I neglect to get rest after a prolonged time of ministering. I have also never been one to frequent the doctor's office. I am in no way implying that something is wrong with going to doctors. I consider them a valuable and a tremendous blessing, especially those that are believers. The many medical advancements we enjoy today, from the successful preventive treatment of the ancient plague of leprosy, to the vaccine for polio, are a testimony of the blessing this profession is to us.

Tenaciously, I stood on the healing scriptures, looking for the healing to come, but things seemed to get worse. Because the pain was constant, the few moments that I was able to catch naps were much too short to get any real rest. I began to dream of relief. For a fleeting moment, I even thought of how sweet leaving this life would be, to escape the unrelenting pain. The phrase *"with his stripes we are healed"* [124] seemed to mock me. Here I was, a teacher of divine healing, who had gotten little to no results. When I could stand it no longer, I reasoned that at least at the hospital they could prescribe medication for relief.

Finally, I decided to drive to the one down the street from the church. With some effort, I got into my car, and on my way began to have flashbacks of the frustrating experiences that I had had with my treatment through the years. It seemed as though I could never adequately explain to doctors what was really wrong, and they could never detect accurately what the problem really was. As I drove, I clearly heard the question, "Do you want to do this, or do you want the Lord to heal you?" I was in so much discomfort that I just wanted out. I didn't want to keep expecting and being disappointed. But I answered, "I want to be healed by the Lord." Nothing had changed, and there was no one around from whom I could seek guidance, but I decided to go back again and take a stand. By this time, I was weary and desperate and very troubled by the realization that what I was doing wasn't yielding results.

WHEN DO YOU BELIEVE YOU ARE HEALED?

We were having an all-night prayer that evening. I entered the church and knelt down in the back. The church was dark and people were praying. I was miserable as I knelt on the floor. I had no idea what to do next except to stand on the scriptures on healing. After being sick for so long I was fed up. I said to the Lord, "I'm back here again, I believe your word. Now, I'm believing for two things from you. First, I need a good night's sleep. Secondly, I need this swelling to go down. But since I've waited so long, normal recovery will not do. I want a miracle." I went back to the scriptures on healing. I said, "I believe with his stripes I'm healed." The Lord said to me, not in an audible voice, but he spoke to me on the inside. "When do you believe you were healed? When?" I saw the point of his question. I said, "I believe I'm healed now! Right now! And I believe from this moment forward everything that happens to me is my healing being manifested!"

Immediately, the devil began to remind me of all the times I had spoken without results. He attempted to bring before me the vision of me pleading to be healed to no avail. But I interrupted him in the middle of his words. I said, "No! No! I believe that everything that happens to me from this moment forward is my healing taking place." It was then that the Lord began to show me how to come out from under this oppression. My head hurt so badly I didn't want to do anything but hold it steady. But he told me to turn my head a certain way and begin to cough. When I began to cough, almost immediately I felt some relief. After a few coughs, I noticed that I was coughing up what was apparently an infection. The more I coughed, the better I felt, and soon I was relieved enough to lie down and sleep.

What a sweet sleep it was, to be relieved from the days and nights of pain. When I awoke the next morning, the pain was gone. Some swelling in my throat remained. Again, the devil began to remind me of my most recent faith failures. He tried his best to tell me it wasn't going to be completed. Again, I spoke sternly, not just for the devil to hear, but also to underscore my new found boldness. I said, "No! No! I said everything that's happening to me from last night onward is my healing. I have asked for two things. I've had my night's sleep, now I will have my miracle." I kept that in my thoughts that morning although nothing had yet manifested. I refused to allow any other thought.

After the all-night prayer, I went upstairs to my apartment to wash up. I stepped in front of the mirror and started to brush my teeth. As I did, a hole appeared in the back of my throat as if someone had made an incision, and I could see what appeared to be the infection, draining out through the hole. It drained until the swelling was all gone. My miracle had come! I felt a joy and a peace that I cannot describe. I had taken a stand and God had come through. I had heard what God had done for others, but this was my own personal miracle. I praised him and thanked him, and testified to anyone who would hear me that God will heal if we will take a stand. Since that time, the Lord has often reminded me of that stand, and of the power of that little word "now."

"Now" is a powerful word that releases faith and puts the devil on notice that from this moment on, I am taking my stand. Hebrews 11:1 states: *"Now faith is the substance..."*

CHAPTER THIRTY TWO

RECEIVE NOW

"Now faith is the substance of things hoped for the evidence of things not seen."

- Hebrews 11:1

Mistaking "hope" for "faith" can be disastrous. But many are unaware of the difference. For clarity, hope is looking for something in the future. Faith is saying, "<u>I believe I receive it now.</u>" Hope is an earnest expectation of a future event. Faith is the confidence that "<u>we have the petition.</u>"[125] Hope is a good waiter, but a poor receiver. Faith is an action word. Hope is like a blueprint for a building. Faith is the action of hammering the nail into the wood, carrying out the plans of the blueprint. The above scripture states: "Now faith is the substance of things hoped for...." Hope is the picture we hold of what shall be. Faith is the action which causes it to come to pass.

Jesus admonished his disciples *"when you pray, believe you receive, and you shall have."*[126] Claiming unseen things is important to the principle of faith. It is called the evidence of things that are not seen, proof that we own something we cannot see. There are a multitude of things that are not seen. The very air we breathe is one of them. Faith is the power God has designed for us to bring those things into our lives. Faith loves to move among the unseen things of life, confident that once he completes his work, the unseen will become seen. Faith, which comes from the heart or spirit of man, recognizes the realm of the spirit first. To faith, the spirit realm is the world that is real. **Faith calls something done as**

soon as it appears in the spirit in line with God's word. The force of faith knows that everything occurs first in that realm. After a period of time has elapsed, it breaks forth into the natural physical world and can be detected by the senses.

There must be a point at which faith is released. Our Father, God, speaks the end from the beginning, and calls things that are not (visible) as though they were.[127] Whether healing, or provisions, or other things we desire, claiming unseen things pleases God. God himself has chosen to remain undetectable to natural senses. We sometimes have a difficult time with it. The inmate who has lived for years in confinement, when released, must relearn to function in the unconfined society. Likewise, after being reborn into the kingdom, we who have been confined to the limitations of the natural "seen" realm must learn to navigate the new turf.

It's quite safe to keep relegating things to the future, but not effective. "I will receive someday in the future" is a very low risk statement. But it does not pull the trigger to the faith weapon. Faith takes it now and refuses anything to the contrary. You must be bold enough to set a time at which faith is released, and claim the thing received. This kind of activity stumps the devil because he is used to defeating man who is limited to the natural realm. With God and man there is no tomorrow. No one lives or works there. God is in the now. He is a right now God. He has never been confined to the time restrictions of his creation. He exists in the eternal now. If you're going to walk in harmony with him, you're going to receive answers now and believe God.

Kenneth Hagin once said, "Hope isn't what causes God to hear your prayer; faith is. If you are only hoping, there will not be an answer to your prayers."

You are waiting on God and God is waiting on you.

SECTION ENDNOTES

SCRIPTURE REFERENCES

SECTION ONE

1. Mark 4:35-41
2. Daniel 10:12-13
3. Psalm 107:20
4. St. John 1:1
5. Hebrews 11:3
6. Ephesians 4:1
7. II Corinthians 4:4
8. Matthew 8:26
9. Matthew 4:4
10. John 4:24
11. II Corinthians 5:17
12. II Corinthians 5:1
13. Matthew 17:20
14. II Corinthians 5:7
15. Hebrews 11:6
16. Proverbs 4:20-22
17. Romans 4:19
18. Galatians 3:26-29
19. Judges 6:14, 36-40
20. Isaiah 55:10
21. Kenneth Copeland paraphrased

SECTION TWO

22. Romans 8:37
23. I Corinthians 15:34
24. Isaiah 53
25. II Corinthians 5:21
26. I John 1:9
27. John 10:10
28. James 1:13
29. James 1:3
30. Matthew 6:13
31. Psalm 105:37
32. Romans 5:12
33. I Pet. 2:24
34. Deuteronomy 28:13

SECTION THREE

35. Proverbs 3:5,6
36. Ephesians 4:26,27
37. II Samuel 15-19
38. Luke 11:17, Living Translation
39. I Corinthians 14:40
40. I Samuel 8:19-22 41. I Samuel 3:13
41. II Peter 1:5&6,10
42. I Peter 3:4, Ephesians 5:16
43. I Kings 19
44. Acts 16:25
45. Psalm 149:6,7

SECTION FOUR

46. Psalm 20:1
47. John 4:24
48. II Cor. 2:9,10
49. Romans 8:14
50. Romans 8:16
51. Romans 8:1
52. I Corinthians 1:27
53. Matthew 13:1
54. John 10:27
55. James 1:5
56. Hebrews 4:2
57. Luke 17:5-10
58. Hebrews 10:38
59. Deuteronomy 28:8
60. Matthew 7:24
61. Isaiah 53:5
62. I John 5:14,15
63. Matthew 7:8
64. Joshua 1:3
65. Numbers 13:31
66. Hebrews 3:11

SCRIPTURE REFERENCES

67. Rom. 8:17
68. John 16:15, Amplified Translation
69. I John 3:2
70. Matthew 18:19
71. Deuteronomy 8:3

SECTION FIVE

72. Mark 16:16
73. Luke 10:19
74. James 4:7
75. Ephesians 4.47
76. Matthew 28:18-20
77. Matthew18:18
78. Ephesians 1:23
79. Ephesians 1:19
80. Ephesians 2:1,6
81. Psalm 84:11
82. Psalm 51:5
83. Proverbs 13:4
84. Psalm 89:34
85. James 4:7
86. Matthew 16:18
87. John 10:10
88. John 8:44
89. I John 5:4
90. Joshua 1:3
91. Jonah 2:7
92. Ephesians 2:6
93. Matthew 13:19
94. Mark 4:39
95. Matthew 4:1-11

SECTION SIX

96. II Peter 1:3
97. Luke 8:5-15
98. Isaiah 55:10
99. Hebrews 4:12
100. Matthew 4:4
101. Ephesians 1:3
102. I John 3:2
103. Matthew 18:19
104. Deuteronomy 8:3
105. John 15:7
106. Mark 11:24
107. Romans10:10
108. Mark 5:34
109. I Samuel 17:46 KJV paraphrased
110. II Corinthians 12:9
111. Matthew 17:20
112. Isaiah 53:5
113. I Samuel 16:25
114. I John 4:18
115. Psalm 1:2 114. James 5:7

SECTION SEVEN

116. Matthew 6:34
117. Romans 6:14
118. Philippians 4:8
119. Matthew11:10
120. Acts 16:6&7
121. Matthew 6:12-15
122. II Corinthians 5:17
123. Matthew18: 22
124. Luke 5:23
125. Isaiah 53:5
126. I John 5:14 126. Mark 11:24
127. Romans 4:17

▪ ABOUT PASTOR AL GEE

With years of experience as a father, pastor, evangelist, convention speaker, teacher and university administrator, Pastor Al Gee has committed his life to empower believers and congregations throughout the world with keys to powerful living and insights to life changing kingdom principles. The Gee family presently resides in Durham, North Carolina.

▪ CONTINUE THE CONVERSATION

Stop by www.algeeministries.com for the latest resources, FREE video clips, and news from Al Gee Ministries.

▪ SPEAKING ENGAGEMENTS

Would you like to bring Pastor Al's empowering message to your congregation? Contact our team at **www.algeeministries.com**.

▪ PARTNER WITH AL GEE MINISTRIES

Together we can make a difference through your prayers and financial gifts. For more information visit us at **www.algeeministries.com** or write us at **P.O. Box 12553, Durham, NC, 27709.**

FOLLOW ME

 www.algeeministries.com   @PASTORALGEE   /ALGEEMINISTRIES

www.ingramcontent.com/pod-product-compliance
Lightning Source LLC
Chambersburg PA
CBHW070429010526
44118CB00014B/1958